A Church, a School

SOUTHERN CLASSICS SERIES
Mark M. Smith and Peggy G. Hargis,
Series Editors

A Church,
a School

Pulitzer Prize–Winning
Civil Rights Editorials from
the *Atlanta Constitution*

Ralph McGill

New Introduction by
Angie Maxwell

THE UNIVERSITY OF SOUTH CAROLINA PRESS

*Published in Cooperation with the Institute for
Southern Studies of the University of South Carolina*

Cloth edition published by Abingdon Press, 1959
Paperback edition published by the University of South Carolina Press,
Columbia, South Carolina 29208

www.sc.edu/uscpress

Manufactured in the United States of America

21 20 19 18 17 16 15 14 13 12
10 9 8 7 6 5 4 3 2 1

Library of Congress Cataloging-in-Publication Data
McGill, Ralph, 1898–1969.
  A church, a school : Pulitzer Prize-winning civil rights editorials from
the Atlanta constitution / Ralph McGill ; new introduction by Angie
Maxwell. — Pbk. ed.
    p. cm. — (Southern classics series)
  "Published in cooperation with the Institute for Southern Studies of the
University of South Carolina."
  Originally published: New York : Abingdon Press, 1959.
  ISBN 978-1-61117-129-7 (pbk. : alk. paper)
1. African Americans—Civil rights—Southern States—History—20th cen-
tury. 2. African Americans—Segregation—Southern States—History—
20th century. 3. Southern States—Race relations—History—20th century.
4. Segregation in education—Southern States—History—20th century.
5. Rule of law—Southern States—History—20th century. I. University of
South Carolina. Institute for Southern Studies. II. Atlanta constitution.
III. Title.
  E185.61.M135 2012
  323.1196'0730904—dc23

                                    2012020576

Publication of the Southern Classics series is made possible in part
by the generous support of the Watson-Brown Foundation.

Contents

CONTENTS

Series Editors' Preface

The pre-civil-rights South was thought to represent all that was wrong with the United States. It was the national exception; it was a national embarrassment. As a crusading journalist, Ralph McGill, however, saw the South and its people for what it and they could be and dedicated more than three decades of his life to exposing the costs of hatred, undermining pernicious regional myths, and educating and enlightening all who read his columns. In *A Church, a School,* his Pulitzer-winning collection of columns from the *Atlanta Constitution,* McGill urged white moderates in the region to turn "their backs on the extremists and the politicians who peddled fear" and to end human injustice, in all its forms. As Angie Maxwell's insightful introduction rightly concludes— we need more Ralph McGills. This Southern Classic reminds us that the good fight is not yet done and that the nation, perhaps now more than ever, needs men and women with the moral courage to expose hatred, to shun incivility, and to protect the fragile freedom of all.

Southern Classics returns to general circulation books of importance dealing with the history and culture of the American South. Sponsored by the Institute for Southern Studies, the series is advised by a board of distinguished scholars who suggest titles and editors of individual volumes to the series editors and help establish priorities in publication.

Chronological age alone does not determine a title's designation as a Southern Classic. The criteria also include significance in contributing to a broad understanding of the region, timeliness in relation to events and moments of peculiar interest to the American South, usefulness in the classroom, and suitability for inclusion in personal and institutional collections on the region.

MARK M. SMITH
PEGGY G. HARGIS
Series Editors

Introduction

"Let Us Now Praise Ralph McGill"

Born at the turn of the century in the East Tennessee hill country that decades earlier had supported the Union cause, Ralph Waldo Emerson McGill spent his career explaining the South to itself. Perhaps his name, given by the beloved doctor who delivered him,[1] set him on an inevitable course of transcendent self-examination. Whatever the source of his unrelenting observation, it proved productive and promising even at a young age. The discipline that gave rise to nearly ten thousand daily columns, syndicated in three hundred newspapers across the country, was perfected in the Marine Corps, but the dissenter in McGill was never silenced. His truth telling proved costly at times. He was suspended and, in turn, did not graduate from Vanderbilt University because he published an article criticizing the administration in the school paper. However, his unflinching pen and his penchant for storytelling landed him a job as a sportswriter at the local *Nashville Banner,* where he honed the craft that would make him famous. In 1929 the *Atlanta Constitution* came calling. McGill was not satisfied by the limitations of the sports beat, and when the *Constitution* assigned him to cover the Cuban Revolt in 1933, McGill entered the world of politics and social justice that became his home for the next three decades.

The Great Depression turned his attention southward again. McGill recognized before many others did, that "under the gray misery of the depression there was the surge of a new tide running, a push toward change, the murmuring of many voices of discontent."[2] According to biographer Harold H. Martin, McGill believed Franklin D. Roosevelt when the president, whom McGill heard speak in Roosevelt's adopted hometown of Warm Springs, "described Georgia as an 'unfinished state'—its growth cut short by the Civil War and the tortured aftermath." From the ashes a southern phoenix could rise as an "instrument of progress."[3] The evolution of the South became the beat of McGill's life. It was a risky choice that many southern journalists did not make. Choosing to look to the war in Europe, others avoided the war at home. And it was a war.

McGill was not an instant activist. His early writing resisted federal intervention into the Jim Crow South. Championing pragmatism, McGill urged patience and feared resurrecting the pain and rage associated with Reconstruction among white southerners. Though, as gradual as his awakening about race was, as noted most recently by Bronwen Dickey,[4] his fist pounded harder every year. Sometimes his knocking, so to speak, was only heard by those who were affected most personally. For example, on the first day he took over as executive editor of the *Constitution,* he ordered the paper to capitalize the *N* in the word *Negro.* According to Martin, several teachers from historically black colleges and universities in Atlanta wrote letters of praise.[5]

As foretold by the title of this daily column, "One More Word," McGill rarely left a world event undiscussed, particularly in the escalating southern march toward equality. His opinions were shaped by his prolific reading habits—multiple daily newspapers and two to three books each week[6]—and by his commitment to authenticity. McGill traveled the South exhaustively, meeting with the subjects of his columns personally. His efforts and his knowledge earned him the moniker the Conscience of the South and brought a responsibility he could not ignore. As a writer he was not immune to the ego's search for praise and validation. As Leonard Ray Teel has noted, in the late 1940s McGill claimed that he deserved a Pulitzer Prize for "placing racial moderation on the South's political agenda."[7] He believed his call for moderation to be radical when compared to the culture of silence on racial issues that competing papers fostered.

But moderation was not radical enough, nor was McGill. The decade of the 1950s transformed the editor into a voice worthy of national audiences. McGill himself has claimed that one singular sentence, uttered at Little Rock Central High School in 1957, revealed the civil rights movement to be an unstoppable force, an inevitable reality. In the crowd that day, McGill heard "the wailing shriek of a segregationist lady: 'Oh, Lordy, the niggers is already in the School.'" Years later McGill reflected on the experience. "Ever since 1957," he confessed, "it has been my belief that [it was] one of the most revealing, and perhaps significant sentences in the history of the move to admit the Negro to the First and Fourteenth Amendment clubs."[8] McGill began to realize that southern leaders had inflamed white southerners beyond acceptance of limited or gradual integration. Massive resistance set in across the South, and McGill's calls for moderation fell on defiant and deaf ears.

His mission had to change. He pushed back against the growing support for violence and self-destruction. His lashed out at the "jackals, the cowards, the haters, the failures who hate achievers, the yapping feist pack that tries to drown out the truth; those who dislike Jews, Negroes, Catholics, 'liberals'; the bitter and evil persons who organize themselves and send out hate literature; the Klan types, the 'States Rights' diehards. . . . They are the abscessed in America's society."[9]

McGill's life was threatened because of the words he wrote. Crosses were burned in his yard. But when a Jewish temple in Atlanta was bombed in 1959, he expounded on the very nature of hate. "Let us face the facts," he stated. "This is a harvest. It is the crop of things sown."[10] That column, titled "A Church, a School," along with those collected in the volume of the same name and here reprinted, earned him the Pulitzer Prize for Editorial Writing.

The Evolution of Ralph McGill

McGill's record on race was by no means perfect; it evolved over time. And even late in his career, there were aspects of the Jim Crow South that, from a present-day viewpoint, expose the limitations of a southern white perspective during this turbulent time. In a column that he wrote for *Reporter Magazine* in June 1960, McGill announced that "Negroes of the Black Belt are in general apathetic about the political aspects of citizenship."[11] McGill, in fact, did not blame African Americans for this perceived apathy; he blamed the systematic oppression that dominated the region and depressed any efforts toward political leadership. Scholars reflecting back on this period now recognize the extensiveness of black participation—just in ways often overlooked or misunderstood by even the most well-intentioned activists, such as McGill. His strength, and the element that allowed for his transformation on the issue of race, was his ability to see the interconnectedness of prejudice. McGill, through his immersion in his southern subject matter, came to understand the way in which disenfranchisement, poverty, and lack of education created an oppressive cycle from which African Americans in the South could not escape. He would teach what he learned to any and all who would listen.

McGill scholar Calvin M. Logue has argued that, over the course of his career, McGill developed six core beliefs that shaped his stances on American life. Three of these beliefs represent McGill in the years prior to explosion of the civil rights movement: "Individuals and governments should pursue policies that are feasible"; "laws should be obeyed"; and "education is requisite to individual and community progress."[12] These dictates were already evident in McGill's early writings on race in the South—in the columns he later described as "pale tea."[13] In the years prior to the landmark *Brown v. Board* (1954) desegregation case, for example, McGill touted the line drawn by southern political leaders and validated by the United States Supreme Court at the turn of the century—that "separate but equal" was a feasible and constitutionally sound practice in the South. He predicted that if segregation was eventually declared unconstitutional, "the majority of Southern Negro children will continue to go to separate schools." And he warned, "The wiser Negro leadership, with segregation no longer sanctioned by law, will be content to maintain separate schools until public opinion accepts it."[14]

But McGill, as he continued to do in the decades that followed, insisted that white southerners be honest about the practice of "separate but equal." He contended repeatedly that southerners were violating the law. "We . . . have repeatedly insisted we want to be fair to the Negro," McGill confessed. "Let us admit that the record shows we have not."[15] The fourth tenet of his personal philosophy—that "all persons should be granted the rights and privileges of full citizenship"—was at play here.[16] But McGill, like many white men of his generation, was able to reconcile this belief with segregation. The "separate but equal" vision was practical, validated by the

Supreme Court, and if obeyed by white southerners would not impinge on the rights of African Americans, or so McGill thought. It was the final two core beliefs, as noted by Logue, that only surfaced when McGill began to realize that his radicalism was radical only to the most conservative pro-segregationists.

It was only when McGill engaged further with the leaders of the movement that he understood the weakness of his moderate stance. Walter White, then president of the NAACP, went so far as to denounce McGill as a "weasel" for his lack of support for a federal antilynching initiative.[17] McGill initiated his campaign by encouraging white southerners to prepare for the inevitability of integration, specifically by breaking the code of silence that surrounded and sustained Jim Crow. Using a familiar character, McGill warned white southerners about emulating Scarlet O'Hara, who,"when confronted with a distasteful decision, pushed it away with the remark, 'we'll talk about it tomorrow.' But 'tomorrow' has an ugly habit of coming around."[18] He cautioned against extreme reactions, reiterating his promise to his readers that any court decision would be implemented slowly: "The court can rule segregation unconstitutional—but allow the states affected a period of years in which to work out procedures satisfying the court's decision. Whatever happens, for some years the majority of Negro children will continue to go to separate schools. . . . The vital part is—there is no reason for violence, whatever the decision. Leadership everywhere in the South must talk about this and make it clear. Anger and violence will solve nothing."[19] Despite his advocacy of nonviolence, McGill's conciliatory tone bears little resemblance to the uncompromising, courageous voice that emerged in the years that followed.

The violent events that rocked the South in the late 1950s and early 1960s clearly influenced McGill to take a stronger public stance on civil rights. In the aftermath of the 1963 bombing of an African American Baptist Church in Birmingham, a Trappist monk wrote to McGill and helped him redefine his vision for the South. According to Harold H. Martin, "the phrase the monk had sent him—*Qui tacer consentire videtu*—meant 'He who is silent is understood to consent.'"[20] McGill, nicknamed the Conscience of the South, now recognized that his own moderation was empowering the segregationists by signaling consent. The revelation led McGill to embrace two final core beliefs. He now knew that "free individuals have a moral responsibility to oppose wrong." And he recognized that slow change meant no change. "Southern states should ensure the rights and privileges of their own citizens,"[21] he believed. And if they didn't, the federal government would have to intervene.

The McGill Method

McGill's evolution was not sudden or abrupt. His writing revealed his mounting frustration with the southern moderate position. But how did the increasingly radical McGill become so influential in the South and syndicated so widely throughout the country? How, in effect, did McGill gain the trust of his white southern readers? In the columns for which he was awarded the Pulitzer Prize, and which are collected in *A Church, a School,* he employed three primary tactics intended to educate and, in turn, to change the minds of white southerners. First and foremost, McGill, in a muckraking spirit, debunked sacred myths about the region, challenging the assumptions that kept white southern culture and the Jim Crow system stagnant. In the title column, "A Church, a

School," McGill recounted that one of the bombers of the Jewish temple in Atlanta had warned a news service of the violent strike, which the bomber said would be carried out by the Confederate Underground. Denouncing the bomber's self-defined connection with the white nationalist organization, McGill pointed to the example of General Lee as a respected Confederate leader who, "time after time . . . urged his students at Washington University to forget the War Between the States and to help build a greater and stronger union" (11). The South did not have to maintain a perpetual backward glance but, rather, could work with the country at large toward progress for all Americans—at least this is how their beloved General Lee would have behaved. In another piece, entitled "General Lee Reminds Us," McGill debunked the myth of the obstinate Confederate die-hard, insisting that Lee understood the implications of war and its impact on the region and, in particular, on "its children of generations to come" (45).

Attempting to refashion an old hero was not McGill's only effort to challenge the mantle of southern white supremacy. He attacked the Ku Klux Klan and the pageantry and history that it claimed. Tackling the Klan's claim to "100-per-cent Americanism"—to be the white, Christian, true Americans—McGill proclaimed that the KKK "prostitutes the cross of Christ by burning it to advertise its meetings and to attract the suckers" (22). He did not mince words, particularly when addressing the way the Klan exploited the Christian faith shared by many southerners. And he specifically noted the way in which the KKK reinterpreted the Bible, "making over the New and Old Testaments" in a manner that "justifies hate and twists the great commandment to love they neighbor as thyself to apply only to 100-per-cent Americans" (22).

McGill was not satisfied merely to debunk the legend of individual southern characters and groups. He also undertook a review of abstract principles that white southerners accepted and resurrected when they sought to justify their behavior. When they championed the cry of states' rights, McGill reminded his readers that southerners had voluntarily delegated much of their autonomy to the federal government. "Since 1865," McGill wrote, "the states have all but abandoned those reserve rights, such as building their own highways, hospitals, health departments, et cetera. They have, of necessity, turned to the central government to take over many state responsibilities" (73). This shift in the system of federalism demanded by the antifederalists in the years following the American Revolution, was not exclusive to the South. But McGill demonstrated the hypocrisy of the massive resistance movement and, specifically, of the call for interposition by state governments against federal authority. Such a stance was as doomed as secession in 1860 had been. In his assessment of the Byrd political machine in Virginia, from which the interposition cry was the loudest, McGill concluded, "Here began the great tragic deception of the Southern people" (82). Political leadership in Virginia and in many other southern states misled their southern constituents into believing that such resistance would be victorious in the war against integration. This failure of leadership initiated the frantic spread of "the dangerous and false theory of interposition and defiance which," McGill noted, "already have brought so much grief to so many Southern people" (82–83).

In the turbulent years following the Supreme Court's desegregation orders in *Brown v. Board* and *Brown v. Board II,* white southerners fell back on the myths that sustained their way of life by resurrecting the Confederate cause, proclaiming the Christian "truth" of the KKK, and arguing for the constitutional authority of states' rights. And when denounced at every turn by critical outsiders and burgeoning internal voices of dissent, many white southerners compiled a list of others to blame for the problems they faced in their hometowns and home states. International agitators and experts were demonized for their influence on the Supreme Court. McGill did not shy away from tackling these myths as well. Swedish sociologist Gunnar Myrdal and his book *An American Dilemma: The Negro Problem and Modern Democracy* were favorite targets of segregationists. In a column aptly titled "Once a Biscuit Is Opened," McGill informed his readers that Myrdal's book was only one of "several publications referred to by the court, not as an authority on law but as one by a man who had studied the effect of unequal application of the laws" (49–50). And he announced to his audience (after noting that most of them had not read Myrdal's work) that "his book does not condemn the South. It argues that the problem is national, not regional" (50). Rather than solely correct misinformation, McGill also offered another suspect in the "crime" of ushering in change to the Jim Crow South. Southern politicians, he wrote, "have opened the Dixie biscuit for industry, labor unions, larger city populations and less rural, and yet they spend much of their time and emotions continually trying to put the biscuit back together again just like it was" (49). Such socioeconomic and demographic shifts did not happen in a vacuum or without repercussions for race relations in the region, McGill explained.

White southerners, however, were blind to the responsibility that their own elected officials played in initiating hysteria among constituents and advocating doomed plans to maintain segregation. Instead, argued McGill, they blamed "outsiders" and "agitators from up North," whom they resented for not understanding "our way of life" (50). The enemy North was an old foe and scapegoat that resurfaced in times of perceived crisis. "In 1860 the South had grown so sensitive to criticism and the apparent denials of its proclaimed virtues that its exasperations led to disaster," warned McGill.[22] The region's problems were of its own making, he argued, and misinformation and southern mythology clouded the vision of many moderates. Providing clarity without ridicule was McGill's method of gaining the trust of his readers and the respect of his national audience.

In addition to tackling the often unquestioned tenets of the white "southern way of life," McGill attempted to garner the support of moderates by exposing the hate of the extremists. The white southern sensitivity to criticism that McGill observed had created a pantheon of enemies that inspired strong emotions. By turning the spotlight on hatred and violence in the South, McGill made it virtually impossible for many southern moderates to maintain their neutrality. In "While the Clock Ticks," McGill summarized this position with the terse statement: "So emotionally committed are most persons in the Deep South that those who do not agree are damned as enemies and worse" (20). McGill watched as this commitment to rage and blame—which was tolerated by southern moderates—intensified in the years after the Supreme Court's desegregation order. McGill knew that this would inevitably give rise to physical violence. In a column titled "Violence Destroys Its Own Purposes," McGill referenced biblical scripture and announced that "what we are getting is the fruit of the tree" (79).

McGill condemned the KKK as a "refuge for scoundrels."[23] He vilified pro-segregation demagogues such as John Kasper, who functioned as a "racist Pied Piper, followed by all those who before had lacked someone to articulate their prejudices, fears, and hates."[24] In a column titled "'Mene, Mene, Tekel, Upharsin'—Daniel," McGill directed his own growing rage at the bombers of the southern landscape.

> The mob, which is hate, always strikes at the church and at the school.
>
> This they have done here. They will likely strike again. Murder and destruction are in their hearts. But for them and the leadership which has encouraged the golden calf of lawlessness, the handwriting is on the walls: "Mene, mene, tekel, upharsin" (Dan 5:25).
>
> Belshazzar didn't live out the night. (13)

"It is night now," McGill proclaimed, and "it may be a long one. But the dynamiters will not live it out" (13). McGill's primary purpose was to make his fellow white southerners unable to reconcile their moderation and silence with their morality. He knew that exposing the most extreme hate would elucidate the moral problem that since the region's inception had been created and cultivated. Years later McGill, reflecting on the KKK, concluded that the organization had one "asset. It forced Southerners to a decision pro or con."[25] In fact that decision was, at least in part, forced by the pen of Ralph McGill.

The final component of McGill's efforts to educate white southerners toward the progressive cause of civil rights required him to interpret the Constitution to a stubborn audience that relied on the misinformation circulated by pundits and repeated by politicians. In column after column in *A Church, a School*, McGill posed as a constitutional law professor, citing founding documents, precedent, and legal philosophy in his battle for nonviolent acceptance of social change.

In "Reverence for the Law," McGill championed the beauty of the founders' design, most notably the insulation of the court from political pressure. He argued for the centrality of the legal system in American government. "Law is our real foundation," he wrote. Pointing to the long-term implications of resistance, he warned, "We cannot exist half lawless and half lawful—anymore than we could be half free and half slave" (29). He discredited the strict constructionists who argued that the Constitution was "meant to protect only the rights, liberties, and concepts of property" (25) as they existed when the Constitution was passed in 1789. And, in the aftermath of the federal showdown at Little Rock Central High School, McGill argued in his column "The Judicial Power" for the finality of Supreme Court decisions: "For the sake of our own thinking we must know that unless there is an amendment to the Constitution the court decision of 1954 is constitutional and binding on the courts, despite sincere disagreement." He added, "We have been hurt enough by those who have said it is unconstitutional" (36).

McGill broke ground when he focused not on the harm that segregation and violence had on its real victims, African Americans, but when he told his white readers how much their resistance and silence hurt themselves—how it stifled their minds and created a cultural lag that would affect their children and their children's children. In his column "Notes on Bastille Day," he warned southern moderates that "if we ever grow sympathetic toward the mob when it opposes the principles of justice and humanity, we too will destroy our system of government" (42). And drawing a parallel to the years preceding the French Revolution, McGill cast white southerners as the facilitators of violence in a morality play that transcended time and country. "In France in 1789 and the bloody years thereafter," he wrote, "the mob and all its outrages were tolerated. The most dreadful demagogues were allowed full sway. Massacre followed massacre" (42). McGill consistently placed blame on the South's own demagogues and on their failure of political leadership. He lamented Arkansas governor Orval Faubus's efforts to maintain segregation at Little Rock Central High School by force, criticizing his behavior as giving "encouragement to those who are described as the lunatic and crackpot fringe" (38). He defended his name calling by explaining that "these persons are so described because they do not reason or think, and because they have no citizenship or reverence for law. For persons and organizations in high places to give support to defiance of the court encourages all criminals" (38–39). Moreover, in "Violence Destroys Its Own Purposes," McGill attacked the lower court judges who publicly proclaimed that they would defy the Supreme Court's desegregation decision. "What do these men think this inspires ignorant and vicious men to do?" McGill asked. He answered: "It encourages them to violence of the sort we are having—bombings. It always does do that. It always will" (79–80).

What is most clear in a reading of McGill's *A Church, a School* is the personal clarity that McGill achieved as an observer of southern racial practices. McGill knew that the middle would not hold. He launched this three-pronged attack—debunking southern myths, exposing hate, and reinterpreting the Constitution—in an effort to pass this clarity on to his readers. His attack knew no limits. State sovereignty, northern aggression, Christianity, and Communism were all subject to his bright unflinching stare. "The cry of states rights by those whose states have failed in their responsibilities to the people," McGill announced, "is less and less valid" (72).

In *The South and the Southerner* (1959), McGill summarized Klan reports for his readers with hope that they could see the way in which misinformation and southern mythology were used to manipulated the masses: "He [the Klan leader] claimed the C. P. [Communist Party] had men all over the state teaching the Negro that he was as good as anyone else and was entitled to vote and that they were being mistreated. He said rabble-rousers from the North had invaded the South and were here for no other purpose than to stir up the Negro and to cause trouble, and eventually it would cause a lot of Negroes to get killed. He also said rich Yankees were spending a large amount of money in the South supposedly to educate the Negro and all they were doing was trying to teach social equality, and in the end they were making trouble for the Southerner and were planting seeds of communism in the Negroes and that over half of the Negroes today are Communists. This he said the KKK was going to fight as long as there was a white man living."[26] Only southern moderates could change the course of southern history. And they could only do so by turning their backs on the extremists and on the politicians who peddled fear. Their efforts could be aided, McGill knew, by the institution of the church if it too would support activism the way its missionaries abroad did. "Christianity cannot afford to be made to appear ridiculous," argued McGill, "—and yet it is." "Even Christians," he continued, "must agree that the long history of foreign missions and the opposition of Christians to acceptance of colored persons in their churches would be the subject of loud, coarse laughter were it not for the by-product of it."[27] The by-product was violence and death of innocent people.

For some southerners McGill's column was the only dissent in a sea of rage and resistance. "It would be helpful, too, if the people would be told the truth," McGill insisted, "however regrettable it may be, and however much it goes against long-established customs and traditions" (48). In "After Schools Close, Then What?," McGill noted that "there are indications that a considerable number of parents and school children never understood that massive resistance would mean that schooling would end" (52). Truth would expose consequences. Truth would force southern moderates from their sheltered hiding places. Truth would expose mob hate and violence and put pressure on politicians advocating resistance at all costs. The costs were high, too high, McGill knew. But the truth was masked by the mythology of the South and mistaken constitutional interpretations and was guarded by those willing to kill to protect white supremacy.

The Lesson of Ralph McGill

Most of Ralph McGill's books are out of print now, and the southern struggle for acceptance of racial progress and equality that they chronicle is often referenced as a completed and successful campaign. There were indeed substantial victories, many of which Ralph McGill helped make possible. But McGill's specific point of view is still needed in the South, and in the country for that matter. In an increasingly partisan political environment, a contemporary voice like McGill's is essential and, unfortunately, is missing. He was, simply put, a teacher, and a tireless one at that. Martin described McGill's legendary work ethic as a "compulsion as strong as hunger, as deep as the need for love."[28] This commitment to his craft, and to his audience, did not waver for nearly fifty years, despite the increasing demands for his time. "When he started," noted Martin, "a daily essay was all that was required of him. He continued it, seven days a week, long after an added burden of travel, speaking, teaching at seminars, sitting in committees of government, and outside writing took so much of his time."[29] His insatiable drive was born out of an ego and a quest for validation, but McGill managed to transform that particular energy toward a cause greater than himself.

McGill would be the first to admit that his early columns were toothless bites at a problem that he did not fully understand. However, the passage of time affords his critics a broader view of his body of work. With rare exceptions, he demonstrated "amazing consistency,"[30] a steady voice in an unsteady time. Reflecting on McGill's point of view, Martin concluded, "He was instinctively for the quiet and humble and poor, and against the arrogant, the powerful, and in general, the right—though he greatly admired the rich who used their wealth with wisdom and compassion and the powerful who used their authority with restraint. He was for the young and flexible of mind, and against the elderly whose thoughts had crystallized."[31] This finely honed perspective was moralistic in a time when few had the courage to define good and evil. More important, in his role as a teacher (and sometimes a preacher, noted Martin), he knew how to keep his readers' attention and their loyalty. Some critics point to McGill's slow evolution on civil rights as an indication of a flawed and tarnished record: he was not aggressive enough when aggression was needed. Martin has stated that McGill "was leading the thinking of his region, but only as far and as fast as his instincts told him he could go without losing his audience."[32] Perhaps this level of self-awareness should be considered McGill's strength, rather than his weakness. Fellow anti–New Deal columnist Westbrook Pegler pegged McGill as "the editor dimly seen and a 'Jim Crow liberal.'"[33] But just as good professors can recognize when they are covering material at too rapid a pace for the majority of their students and can, in turn, halt and review, so too did McGill with his readers. For some, like Pegler and White of the NAACP, he did not get there fast enough. But he got there, and he towed countless white southerners along with him. McGill recognized that "to understand the South was to know it was in transition."[34] He chose not to "abandon his embattled southern constituency, which he hoped would grow," and which "he hoped would turn from the ranting of demagogues."[35] It was not an easy choice. It was, in fact, a personal gamble that required self-discipline, patience, and an elevation of the collective over the individual. In "While the Clock Ticks," he reminded his readers, "One's personal feelings, however strong, are not relevant to the over-all duty" (20).

McGill's patience was partnered by his ability to place the changing dynamics of American and southern society within a larger historical framework, making his readers recognize that their struggle was, in fact, not unique. He cautioned white readers not to blame contemporary enemies (in this case, Communism) for the movement by African Americans to assert their Fourteenth and Fifteenth Amendment rights. "This aspiration on the part of the Negro citizenship," argued McGill, "would exist if there were no Russia, just as Arab nationalism was in full cry in 1916 before there was a Communist revolution in the Czar's Russia" (68). The South's racial problem, he professed in "A Lesson We Can Learn," "is an old one. It has grown . . . steadily across the bygone years" (68). Citizens in India faced the same struggle against discrimination, and in "Nehru Speaks for the U.S.," McGill compared the two struggles: "In both India and the United States it has been demonstrated that laws are not enough. The answer must come from within, by its own thought, deduction, and will. In both countries what goes on amounts to a revolution, and revolutions must be lived through so that when they do end there will be a status which the people accept. Only in this manner can there be an end to human injustice in a free society" (18). He dared to define the civil rights movement as exactly what many activists knew it to be—a revolution. And he knew enough world history to recognize the need for revolution and to promise his readers that they would survive the changes to their way of life that many of them thought unimaginable. While denouncing the resistance efforts of several states that chose to close public schools in the wake of the Supreme Court's desegregation order, McGill attempted to characterize desegregation and the shifting cultural dynamics of the South as part of a larger and far-reaching wave of change that would define the twentieth century. In "Educate Only the Well to Do?," McGill cautioned that the twentieth century was "the era of great scientific advances and new technologies. It is the time of increasing urbanization. It is a period when more educated people, not fewer, are needed" (63). Surely white southerners would not want their children to fail to compete with the graduates of other regions, McGill reasoned.

Such reasoning, McGill thought, forced his readers to see the consequences of their actions, whether moderate or reactionary. Not only was he able to frame the struggle for African American equality as part of a larger progressive movement afoot in the world, McGill also painted a very stark image of the South were it to remain stagnant. In the foreword to Margaret Anderson's *The Children of the South* (written in 1958 but first published in 1966), a manuscript devoted to young African Americans who fought in the movement, McGill detailed this gap. "The South," he wrote, "has been sacrificing generations of its children." "The results," he continued, "are visible in educational and economic lags as well as in the area of moral convictions and in religious health." "The costs," he confessed, "will be paid for a long time."[36] McGill was not content to mark the loss of status for white citizens. He empathized with the black victims of segregation, noting that this lag had left them with a "handicap that even today is not quite fully understood." He argued that "segregation deadened initiative" and "suppressed personal confidence."[37] And when it came to writing about the young people in the movement, McGill's praise was unabashed. Anderson's book gave him the opportunity to express this praise specifically toward young African Americans for their "dignity and bravery . . . in moments and hours of terror when adults had lost their reason and were made with the poison of hates." Regarding the praise, McGill insisted: "They earned it."[38]

In column after column, McGill humanized African Americans for his readers. But he chose not to champion only the direct victims of segregation; rather McGill often injected his columns with hope and optimism that proved attractive to moderate white southerners who were increasingly wary of the violence erupting around them. He appealed to their sense of manners, insisting that his "raising" required him to show a certain level of respect and reverence to the "Supreme Court and its place in our life, for the Presidency as an office, and for the Congress as the voice and representation of the people" (28). He believed that their national patriotism could trump their loyalty to a segregated South. "The dream of those who made the American Revolution," he noted in the first chapter of The South and the Southerner, "was that this country would, through the years, give to all the world its own freedom and its own faith."[39] Southern racial practices diminished the bright light of American exceptionalism, or so McGill thought. As a command of sorts, McGill told his readers: "We learned that to export our revolution of freedom we had to live it."[40] Framed in this way, white southerners were not the subject of a revolution, they were part of a revolution that the founding fathers had set in motion centuries earlier.

Perhaps McGill wanted to believe that white southerners were capable of change—that truth would, in fact, free them from the control of demagogues and from their own violent and oppressive notions of equality. Or perhaps his personal loyalty to the South clouded his judgment: "Let us say to the world, we love this crippled child which is the South; crippled by a war hard fought and lost, crippled by the tariffs and rates you set when you made the laws, crippled by being made a supplier of raw materials to the industrial East. . . . We love her with a passion and pride you will never understand. But we are fighting for her now. We are fighting to make her well and strong. And we will not much longer be fooled by false prophets of prejudice and fake words and fears."[41] McGill's true intentions may not be known, and he undoubtedly questioned his optimism at times. He insisted that "millions of Southerners who strongly support segregation and who would do all that is possible to retain it, are not willing to tear down the government with violence and anarchy."[42] Biographer Teel argued that McGill wrote that specific statement and many others like it "in faith and hope that it was fundamentally true. . . . He hoped to appeal to the admirable characteristics in the mind and face of the South."[43]

The lesson of Ralph McGill is that hope and truth can bend the stiffest branch. McGill, himself, found power in his own transformation. He knew that "nothing in the South is left un-changed by the changes which are occurring." And he knew that such change could only occur if people could find com-mon ground. He made emotional and cerebral appeals to his readers, and he demanded that they "read and learn."[44] When Ralph McGill died in 1969, Albert M. Davis, the past president of the NAACP in Atlanta, proclaimed that McGill "interpreted the voice of all people who suffered, not only Negroes, but all people who wanted freedom. He was the only voice we had for 25 years."[45] On the day he died, McGill spoke to a group of high school students, railing against apathy and begging them to engage in the world that had been created for them. He was, according to Logue, "impatient with persons who failed to try."[46] They were the generation who could take advantage of the sacrifices that the youth in the movement had made on their behalf. Those activists haunted McGill. "You wake," he wrote, "and remember them all, wondering how their des-tinies worked out; how many escaped."[47] Ralph McGill did not employ scare tactics. He did not demonize the ignorant or vilify those who needed his leadership the most. He did not nurse his own political agenda. His is the voice that is miss-ing in American politics today. And his words continue to have meaning beyond the context in which they were writ-ten, and thus they should be read over and over again. They are reprinted here and are as important and relevant today as they were in 1959. Equality. Reverence. Nonviolence. Read and learn. Read and learn. Read and learn. As McGill himself observed, "A people that loses its self-respect is easily demor-alized and made afraid. They become willing to barter away their ideals and integrity. Such persons can't help us. We need faith and idealism for the long, testing pull that is ahead."[48]

Notes

1. Ralph McGill, *The South and the Southerner* (Boston: Little, Brown, and Company, 1963), 48. Waldo was eventually dropped from his name by "mutual consent," according to McGill.

2. Harold H. Martin, *Ralph McGill, Reporter* (Boston: Little, Brown, and Company, 1973), 39.

3. Ibid., 40.

4. Bronwen Dickey. "Southern Enemy Number One: Ralph McGill and the Burden of History," *Oxford American* 66 (September 2009): 126.

5. Martin, *Ralph McGill*, 81.

6. Dickey, "Southern Enemy," 127.

7. Leonard Ray Teel, *Ralph Emerson McGill: Voice of the Southern Conscience* (Knoxville: University of Tennessee Press, 2001), 255.

8. Ralph McGill, quoted in ibid., 313.

9. Ralph McGill, quoted in ibid., 280.

10. Ralph McGill, *A Church, a School* (New York: Abingdon Press, 1959; Columbia: University of South Carolina Press, 2012), 9. References hereafter will be given parenthetically in text.

11. Reprinted in Ralph McGill, "New Law, Old Fears," in *No Place to Hide: The South and Human Rights* ([Macon, Ga.]: Mercer University Press, 1984), 2:331.

12. Calvin M. Logue, ed., *Southern Encounters: Southerners of Note in Ralph McGill's South* (Macon, Ga.: Mercer University Press, 1983), 6.

13. Ralph McGill, quoted in Dickey, "Southern Enemy," 129.

14. Martin, *Ralph McGill*, 277.

15. Ralph McGill, quoted in Dickey, "Southern Enemy," 128.

16. Logue, *Southern Encounters*, 6.

17. Dickey, "Southern Enemy," 129.

18. Ralph McGill, quoted in Teel, *Ralph Emerson McGill*, 259.

19. Ralph McGill, quoted in ibid., 261.

20. Martin, *Ralph McGill*, 196.

21. Logue, *Southern Encounters*, 6.

22. Ralph McGill, "South of the Dream: Review of C. Vann Woodward's *The Burden of Southern History*," in *No Place to Hide*, 2:338.

23. McGill, *The South and the Southerner*, 144.

24. Ralph McGill, foreword to *The Children of the South*, by Margaret Anderson (New York: Farrar, Straus and Giroux, 1966), x.

25. McGill, *The South and the Southerner*, 144.

26. Ibid., 139.

27. Ralph McGill, "Let's Lead Where We Lag," in *No Place to Hide*, 2:386.

28. Martin, *Ralph McGill*, 301.

29. Ibid.

30. Ibid.

31. Ibid.

32. Ibid., 132.

33. Ibid.

34. Teel, *Ralph Emerson McGill*, 303.

35. Ibid.

36. McGill, foreword to *The Children of the South*, xii.

37. Ibid.

38. Ibid., ix.

39. McGill, *The South and the Southerner*, 18.

40. Ibid.

41. Ralph McGill, quoted in Martin, *Ralph McGill*, 84.

42. Teel, *Ralph Emerson McGill*, 310.

43. Ibid.

44. Ibid., 251.

45. Albert M. Davis, quoted in Dickey, "Southern Enemy," 130.

46. Logue, *Southern Encounters*, 3.

47. Ralph McGill, quoted in ibid.

48. Ralph McGill, quoted in ibid.

A Church, a School

A Church, a School

DYNAMITE in great quantity ripped a beautiful temple of worship in Atlanta. It followed hard on the heels of a like destruction of a handsome high school at Clinton, Tennessee.

The same rabid, mad-dog minds were, without question, behind both. They are also the source of previous bombings in Florida, Alabama, and South Carolina. The schoolhouse and the church were the targets of diseased, hate-filled minds.

Let us face the facts. This is a harvest. It is the crop of things sown.

It is the harvest of defiance of courts and the encouragement of citizens to defy law on the part of many Southern politicians. It will be the acme of irony, for example, if any one of four or five Southern governors deplore this bombing. It will be grimly humorous if certain state attorneys general issue statements of regret. And it will be quite a job for some editors, columnists, and commentators, who have been saying that our courts have no jurisdiction and that the people should refuse to accept their authority, now to deplore.

It is not possible to preach lawlessness and restrict it.

To be sure, none said go bomb a Jewish temple or a school. But let it be understood that when leadership in high places in any degree fails to support constituted authority, it opens the gates to all those who wish to take law into their hands.

There will be, to be sure, the customary act of the careful drawing aside of skirts on the part of those in high places. "How awful," they will exclaim. "How terrible. Something must be done."

But the record stands. The extremists of the citizens' councils, the political leaders who in terms violent and inflammatory have repudiated their oaths and stood against due process of law have helped unloose this flood of hate and bombing.

This too is a harvest of those so-called Christian ministers who have chosen to preach hate instead of compassion. Let them now find pious words and raise their hands in deploring the bombing of a synagogue.

You do not preach and encourage hatred for the Negro and hope to restrict it to that field. It is an old, old story. It is one repeated over and over again in history. When the wolves of hate are loosed on one people, then no one is safe.

Hate and lawlessness by those who lead release the yellow rats and encourage the crazed and neurotic who print and distribute the hate pamphlets—who shrieked that Franklin Roosevelt was a Jew—who denounce the Supreme Court as being Communist and controlled by Jewish influences.

This series of bombings is the harvest, too, of something else.

One of those connected with the bombing telephoned a news service early Sunday morning to say the job would be done. It was to be committed, he said, by the Confederate Underground.

The Confederacy and the men who led it are revered by millions. Its leaders returned to the Union and urged that the future be committed to building a stronger America. This was particularly true of General Robert E. Lee. Time after time he urged his students at Washington University to forget the War Between the States and to help build a greater and stronger union.

For too many years now we have seen the Confederate flag and the emotions of that great war become the property of men not fit to tie the shoes of those who fought for it. Some of these have been merely childish and immature. Others have perverted and commercialized the flag by making the Stars and Bars, and the Confederacy itself, a symbol of hate and bombings.

For a long time now it has been needful for all Americans to stand up and be counted on the side of law and the due process of law—even when to do so goes against personal beliefs and emotions. It is late. But there is yet time.

"Mene, Mene, Tekel, Upharsin"---Daniel

DECENT citizens felt better knowing the Federal Bureau of Investigation was at work in the investigation of the dynamiting of the Atlanta Temple. They were grateful to President Eisenhower for ordering the FBI on the job.

Clues were few. The depraved, callous men who placed the heavy load of explosives at the back of the Temple were without question experts in dynamiting. For them it was a simple job. In their hands the work of destruction could be done without much likelihood of leaving clues.

It is safe to say the investigation will be relentless and thorough. We somehow believe that the luck of these evil persons in escaping will run out. There is no doubt but that the bombing of schools and churches is being directed by one group. They have committed these acts of violence in Tennessee, in North Carolina, in Florida, and in Alabama. The search will go on. One day it will end with the arrest of the guilty.

The community is ashamed. It is distressed and shocked by the dynamiting of the Temple. It is distressed because the state's political leadership has been of the sort which has created a climate of incitement to fanatics and extremist persons, many of whom are neurotic to the point of mental instability. The record on that is clear.

Meanwhile, those who feel impelled to make some tangible expression of their feelings might well do so by sending a contribution to the Temple.

There is a simple, yet touchingly symbolic story about the dynamiting. The inner light, which burns always as the symbol of eternity, was not blasted out by the tremendous explosion which broke a glass window in a neighboring house.

Whether one calls it an accident or a meaningful thing, it is a symbolic fact. The light of truth continues to burn. Public officials may encourage the mob and cause dynamiters to dare to vent their brutal attitude toward religion and education. But the eternal verities remain.

The mob, which is hate, always strikes at the church and at the school.

This they have done here. They will likely strike again. Murder and destruction are in their hearts. But for them and the leadership which has encouraged the golden calf of lawlessness, the handwriting is on the walls: "Mene, mene, tekel, upharsin." (Dan. 5:25.)

Belshazzar didn't live out the night.

It is night now, in Atlanta, and it may be a long one. But the dynamiters will not live it out.

Bombing at Clinton Harms Entire South

B OMBS set off in the school at Clinton, Tennessee, did damage all through the South. That the bombers were financed and their work planned by one of the lunatic fringe extremist organizations, such as once financed the mob-and-bombing inciter John Kasper, cannot be doubted.

There had been no violence at the Clinton school. Not a single incident had marred its orderly activities. This was more than the fanatics could endure; so they reacted with their usual weapon—violence.

Governor Frank Clement, in making available the highest possible reward and offering the FBI all possible assistance, said that the choice was one of education by democratic means or by dynamite. He is correct. The whole South will suffer from this violence. It will not cease to reverberate until many, many months have passed.

Some states, possibly four, have chosen to close their public schools when and if presented with a court decree. That is their right. The federal government cannot and will not interfere.

But those Southern states which have chosen another course must certainly be allowed to proceed without violence from dissenting sources. We should not lose sight of the fact that it was the initial mob violence at Little Rock which precipitated the present crisis in education by making necessary many court cases and decisions which would not have come for a long period of time but for the mobs.

Bombs and violence will further drive national opinion to support the court. Congress is certainly in no mood to endorse mobs and bombs. It will assuredly do nothing to curb the court.

Rather, it may strengthen its policy with legislation. The great majority of American people—including Southern people—want whatever is done to be done within the law. Schools may be closed or kept open—legally. Either course is open to the people involved.

No matter what our attitude toward the segregation question, we cannot condone anarchy and defiance of due process of law.

Nehru Speaks for the U.S.

PRIME Minister Nehru is the greatest voice in Asia, if not the only one.

He raised his voice in his own parliament at Delhi to speak on the problem of racial discrimination in the United States. What he said proves once again that he is a true friend of all that is best in the United States. His voice carries great weight, and it is an honest one. This adds to the importance of what he said.

The United States, said Nehru, wants to solve the problem of racial discrimination, and public opinion is helping in the solution.

He then spoke of his own country's problem. There the question is not one of race, but of caste. He said, in asserting that the United States is making an honest effort, that India's own hands "were not very clean in this respect."

India long ago adopted legislation, at the behest of the late Mahatma Gandhi, to outlaw caste. Both nations have laws against discrimination. No civilized people can support anything else which permits discrimination by one human being against another. To take this stand does not require a belief in the brotherhood of man, but a belief in simple decency and justice.

It is enormously important to us that Nehru should have so spoken. For years the Communists have been having a field day denouncing the United States for what it calls hypocrisy—for proclaiming that we are a democratic nation with liberty and equal justice for all. No nation, of course, exactly meets that standard. But we who have proclaimed it and written it into our laws and our Constitution have offered ourselves as an example.

Our Communist enemies have attacked our claim of freedom and liberty for the individual by sneering that we do not practice what we preach.

They have taken the wild and vicious words of our worst race baiters and put them on the radios of every Asian nation. They have exaggerated and distorted every incident of racial violence. We know these to be the exception. The Communists make them the rule.

They have taken the abusive attacks by the Ku Klux element on the American ministers, senators, the President of the United States, editors, lecturers, and governors of decency and courage and spread them abroad as representing the real heart and soul of America.

It is difficult for truth to catch up with a lie. And so, the extremist racist element in America has been the greatest friend Red Communism has in its attacks on the United States.

Therefore, for the most respected voice in Asia to say calmly, quietly, but forthrightly, that the United States wants to solve its problems of discrimination and is being helped by public opinion, will be a blow to Indian Communists. It should be helpful outside the boundaries of that country.

India has a grave problem—so does the United States.

Both honestly are trying to do what is right—from the viewpoint of Christianity or any ethical standard which may be the standard for other peoples.

In both India and the United States it has been demonstrated that laws are not enough. The answer must come from within, by its own thought, deduction, and will. In both countries what goes on amounts to a revolution, and revolutions must be lived through so that when they do end there will be a status which the people accept. Only in this manner can there be an end to human injustice in a free society.

There are great forces loose in the world today. There are great decisions in the making. We cannot avoid participation in these decisions. The witless ones who think the answer is abuse of the President, of the court, and of all those who try to live by law, can do nothing save add to our eventual sorrow.

Charged as the problem is with emotionalism and prejudice, which feed on ignorance, it is indeed difficult to express any view which points the way toward progress.

Nehru has done it.

While the Clock Ticks

IT is obvious that ahead of the Deep-South states is a chaotic educational period in which some schools will be closed and so-called private schools will attempt to operate.

That a certain amount of chaos will prevail and that injunctions and suits will be commonplace is inevitable.

The Arkansas plan, which a late 1959 Supreme Court decision rendered all but impotent, largely followed that of Georgia, Mississippi, and South Carolina. It allowed the state government to withdraw all state funds and forbade the use of local funds. Georgia's law goes further than others and makes it a felony to attempt to operate a school with locally raised funds.

In general, these states plan to close the buildings and officially declare them no longer available for public schools. They then will proceed to lease the buildings to private operators. The states also have stand-by laws authorizing the governor to pay state funds to children with the provision that the money be used for "education." While no state seems to have spelled this out, the present idea is that in general it would be the amount spent by the state on a per-pupil basis.

Some very good lawyers say that this is so plainly a deliberate evasion of the court's constitutional interpretation as to be illegal on its face. Others say that if the

19

state provides money and leases the buildings it is then in the school business and would be engaged unconstitutionally. Of course, there are many lawyers, especially those who most bitterly assail the court, who argue that such evasions are legal.

Until final judgment none may say which is right, though the 1959 decision in Arkansas indicates these plans are, in general, unconstitutional.

Meanwhile, it is difficult for a newspaper, television, or radio commentator to write or speak in this field except in terms extreme or in weakling vagaries. So emotionally committed are most persons in the Deep South that those who do not agree are damned as enemies and worse.

The fact remains that even in so torrid a climate there is a place for the moderate or the person who believes in due process of law.

To take such a stand is not at all to be "for" or "against" segregation. One's personal feelings, however strong, are not relevant to the over-all duty. Thousands of such persons have held to this position. Many of them are strongly against the court decision. They strongly dislike the idea of desegregation. They may be Christians who cannot reconcile discrimination. They may be persons who say, "I hate the court decision. I wish it had never been made. But I am an American, and I will put my country's institutions above my personal likes and dislikes."

To say that such persons are "for" integration is not the truth. It is a distortion of the facts. How many are there? In the 1958 Virginia election some 33 per cent of the vote went against the winner in an all-out campaign based on the issue. In Arkansas Governor Faubus received about 67 per cent of the vote, and of the 33 per cent opposed to him an estimated 12 per cent was Negro. One may be sure that few of these were "for" school desegregation. They responded to what to them seemed a higher duty.

Sulphuric denunciations of the court and "Ike" accomplish nothing at all.

The person whose love for his state and region includes its future, and who knows even a little history, is aware that at least forty-one of the states have met, or are seeking to meet the issue with due processes of law. In time their representatives in the Congress will act on the issue. Those who offer merely defiance owe a duty to their people to let them know what the price will be.

Hence, in the Deep-South states which plan to close their schools as district by district they become subject to court order, there ought to be alternatives for education if the ill-defined private plan is not constitutional. Voluntary agreements, local school-board autonomy, or other state-wide plans seem to be indicated. To close the schools is certainly legal. But the responsibility of leadership would seem to indicate something other than waiting for chaos to descend.

To believe this is not to be "for" or "against" the court but is, without question, strongly "for" one's state, region, and country.

Kluxers Flee Americans

YES, sir, you can count on the 100-per-cent Americans! They can spot the pretenders to Americanism with an unfailing eye. A group of these 100-per-cent Americans, Lumbee or Croatan Indians, chased the Ku Klux pretenders to Americanism into the swamps, over the hills, and across the dales. It was, altogether, one of the most hilarious and satisfying incidents of recent years.

The Klan, which prostitutes the cross of Christ by burning it to advertise its meetings and to attract the suckers, also exploits Americanism. By paying a necessary sum a fellow can become a 100-per-cent American. The Ku Klux mentality also prostitutes the Christian religion by making over the New and Old Testaments into a KKK revised version. This justifies hate and twists the great commandment to love thy neighbor as thyself to apply only to 100-per-cent Americans, excluding most Protestants, all Roman Catholics and Jews, and all colored peoples. To the Kluxer mentality the Christian communion cup must be a Dixie cup.

Their claim to 100-per-cent Americanism is their major one. And it is entertaining, indeed, to read that in their first encounter with American Indians they fled in panic. The Indians were concerned about encroachment on human rights—their rights.

In this battle of the flying coattails, the Klan leader flung down his sacred banner.

Simeon Oxendine, son of the mayor of Pembroke, community leader, commander of the Veterans of Foreign Wars, who flew on thirty bombing missions over Germany, took the deserted Kluxer flag into Charlotte and walked into the leading hotel lobby wearing it like a scarf.

"It's mine," said Chief Oxendine, who had done more fighting for his country than all the Kluxers put together. "And it will never fly over America if I can prevent it"—to which every truly 100-per-cent American will say "Amen."

There always is the yapping, sometimes snarling, feist-pack to cry "Nazi" or "Red" at those who stand for human rights and who persist in affirming that for Christians the great commandment has validity. But history moves on, and history gives answer to them.

The second chapter in this astonishing story of Indians on the warpath in the year 1958 is that the sheriff of the county sought an indictment against the Kluxers for inciting riot. It was they who pushed into the Indian domain against advice of the law-enforcement officers, and the fact the Indians fired into the air, and not at the Kluxers, doesn't change the story.

The Lumbee Indians have supplied a moment of laughter to a continuing story which has been somber, if exciting. They also have provided an example of forthright and effective action against un-American mob action. North Carolina is a much healthier place, and the air smells sweet, because of the coattail war.

A dip into a North Carolina guide reveals that the

Indians make up one fourth of the population of Robeson County, the largest and one of the more prosperous counties in the United States. It early had its own health and agricultural departments. Its first settlers were English, French, and Scottish Highlanders.

Lumberton, the county seat, lies on both sides of Lumber River, to which settlers gave the name Drowning Creek. The Indian name was Lumbee.

Raleigh sent out in 1587 a colony of one hundred settlers, including seventeen women and nine children. They settled at Roanoke Island. The commander, John White, returned to England. In 1590 he returned to find only a few pieces of broken, rusting armor and carved on one tree the word "Croatan" and on another the letters CRO. The rest was—and to this day is—silence.

A romantic legend has it that these Indians at Lumbee are descendants of that last colony which, starving and ill, either was taken by the Indians or joined them.

That is legend.

But it is a 100-per-cent fact that the real 100-per-cent Americans believe in decent Americanism.

The Oldest Constitution

IT was 1789 when the present Constitution of the United States went into effect.

That it was meant to protect only the rights, liberties, and concepts of property, and the relationships of the states to the nation as they then existed is, of course, not true. There are some, disturbed by the effort to make the rights of citizens to apply equally, who today seem to be arguing that. But even they grow increasingly uncertain.

We are reminded of our Constitution by the news of the day, both at home and abroad. General de Gaulle's struggle to have the Algerians accept and live under the new French constitution is a case in point.

It was also 1789 that the French States-General determined to be a national assembly and began the business of providing France with a constitution.

Since then France has had at least eleven constitutions. The American Constitution has been amended, though with great infrequency, but it still is basically the same old Constitution of 1789. Indeed, with perhaps two exceptions, that dealing with prohibition and the repeal thereof, the amendments have all strengthened the fundamentals of the Constitution.

The Algerians are reluctant to come under the eleventh constitution of France because they wish independence or they lack a belief that their rights would be equal to those of the French.

In the United States we believe in our rights as Americans. This is one reason why any amendment to the Constitution giving the states exclusive control will have very little chance of being adopted by the Congress or the people. If, for example, a state had, as has been proposed, complete control over all aspects of education, all sorts of objectionable possibilities would present themselves. A state with a great preponderance or majority of one religious belief could then say that all schools would teach that faith.

In the field of science, one state might rule, as some following the Scopes trial in Tennessee in the twenties, that some form of science could not be taught because it was contrary to the biblical interpretation held by the state legislature and the people.

Once a state is given absolute control, and the protection of the Constitution is nullified, then it is possible for many things to be done to the rights of a citizen. This is a dangerous field and is precisely why the founding fathers made it difficult to amend the Constitution.

The Constitution of the United States has endured because of the acceptance by the overwhelming mass of the people of the authority of the federal government as being right. The exercise of authority may not always be palatable. But it is accepted. This is the only way orderly government may be had. Our Constitution has been successful for that reason. Only once did it fail—and the price of this was the War Between the States.

The United States has changed profoundly. The Constitution has not. It is a rigid Constitution only as to human rights. When written it did not anticipate giant industry, the atomic bomb, social security, selective service, federal aid to highways, or the wonders and dangers of modern technology and communications.

All soul-and-anger-stirring projects can be debated, discussed, rejected, accepted—without abolishing the old Constitution and getting a new one.

"The government" and its "Constitution" cannot have a rival (in the sense of equal) source of power.

France—and many other countries which have adopted written constitutions—have abolished them over and over again because they did not "fit" some great issue. Our Constitution cannot be said to have been tailored for the past, present, or future, save in the general terms of the rights of citizens. That's why amendments touching on rights, or offering possible abridgment of them, are so carefully considered and find passage so difficult.

Reverence for the Law

A T a meeting of the American Bar Association in Atlanta, Georgia, laymen were invited to attend the sessions and to participate in a lengthy panel program. Under discussion were suggestions by laymen which, in their opinion, might be of assistance to court and judicial procedures.

This is according to the American system, and good will come of it. In fact, good has come of it, as this has been a policy of the A.B.A. for the past several years.

Perhaps because of my "raising," I have had from boyhood what amounts to a reverence for the Supreme Court and its place in our life, for the Presidency as an office, and for the Congress as the voice and representation of the people.

In our time, elected officials too often consider that government belongs to them, rather than the people. The court and the people must continually guard against that.

The Presidency and the Congress, given areas of power by the Constitution, continually contend one with the other. There is jealousy and there is necessary alertness. A weak president can distort the functions of government. The Congress always will seize the reins if they become loosely held by a president. Of course, a listless Congress allows a strong president too much power.

As has been so often pointed out, our government rests

on a three-legged stool—the Court, the Congress, and the Executive. Of the three, the Supreme Court alone is not subject to political or economic pressures of any sort. Its members do not need to seek votes or compromise principles for political support. This fact has seemed always to me the major achievement of the founding fathers. They provided checks and balances against the court. But they were wise beyond their knowing in making it free of the pressures which beat continually on the Presidency and the Congress.

We are a nation of law, and our government is one of politics. The Presidency is not an office separated from pressures. It is a political office. It must be so. It was wise to make it so.

Those Americans who sometimes yearn for someone other than a politician to fill the office are astonishingly naïve. If filled by a man who does not understand politics it does not and cannot function as the framers of the Constitution intended.

Not until President Eisenhower, for example, learned some politics was he able to give strength to his policies. Indeed, he still is handicapped by the fact he feels he must keep as far from politics as possible.

Law is our real foundation. We cannot exist half lawless and half lawful—anymore than we could be half free and half slave.

It is in the American pattern to criticize any branch of our government and to disagree with its findings. But nothing has been more shameful in our time than the attack on the Supreme Court by those extremists who are so fanatic in their opinions they charge the court with being under Communistic influences. They are well aware that this is a preposterous falsehood, utterly without substance. Yet, many uninformed persons have been led to believe it by angry politicians whose very existence as politicians depends on the strength of our three divisions of government.

If these reckless opportunists ever succeed in destroying public confidence in any one branch of our government they then destroy themselves and representative government along with it.

In the last half of the twentieth century it was no longer possible for the courts of this land to say it was constitutional to discriminate against any American citizen. We are either citizens or we are not. To hold a strongly dissenting opinion to this statement and to voice it is an undisputed right. But to cry it down with reckless attacks on the integrity of our court is dangerous and unpardonable.

Here, it seems to me, the American Bar Association is vulnerable to criticism. Its members, above all others, in the past should have reacted strongly to this folly, and in the present should be the more emphatic.

Brooklyn, Little Rock

FROM a Washington, D.C., notebook: What does the administration think of the school problems and issues as produced by Little Rock and the juvenile violence in New York schools?

There is, of course, no official analysis. But from conversations in the capital with those who should know the general administration thinking, it would be something like this:

"There is not, and has not been, any desire to ram anything down the throats of people. There was not, and is not, anything the government can do save to insist on due process of law. This would mean, it is explained, no insistence on an immediate breakdown of the almost century-old traditions and customs. But it would mean, because the government could mean nothing else, acceptance of the principle, and a beginning.

"The arguments, however factual, by Southerners that there is segregation and discrimination in the North, are nothing more than the old exercise of pointing out the motes and beams in each other's eyes. They are a debate in morality but have no bearing whatever on the legal principle involved, or on the necessary policy of support of due process of law. Physical defiance of this due process of law, which is defiance of the orderly processes of government, cannot, and will not, be condoned at Little Rock, or at any point north, south, east, or west.

"This was what happened in Little Rock. It was not what happened in New York's Brooklyn school troubles where due process of law was observed.

"The South certainly has a right, if it wishes, to close down its schools. Certainly Southerners have every right to seek a reversal, or reinterpretation of the Supreme Court decision, and criticize or deplore it as one feels.

"But, there is no question but that the administration leaders feel this should be done within the framework of law and by use of legal measures which are available. This was not what was done at Little Rock. It still is the issue in that Arkansas capital. There the school board on its own initiative had itself proposed a plan to the court. The NAACP opposed it. The court accepted it. All this legal maneuvering took about two years. Then, when a due process order had been made, violence was injected to stop the orderly process of government. This cannot be condoned by any government, in any section."

There also was the feeling that the attempt to represent the Brooklyn school violence as springing from basic racial factors, or as being "like Little Rock," was skillful politics, effectively used, but it was demonstrably non-sense. Claims that Brooklyn's school violence flowed out of segregation in the North have some validity, but are a gross oversimplification. Administration voices point out that in the New York schools the equal rights of the citizen are established and protected. The violence in Brooklyn was not against these rights but against individuals.

It was my feeling the administration feels that the North cannot in conscience adopt a smug attitude in discussing the problem. There *are* motes and beams.

Sociologists and criminologists have studied the Brooklyn problem—and had before violence erupted. They can demonstrate there is a direct relation between criminal acts of violence and crowded, squalid housing; poverty; illiteracy; broken, drunken homes; and working mothers. Another major factor is the frustration caused by absence of opportunity for social or economic improvement in life. In New York it is the Negro and the Puerto Rican who live under more of this burden than others, though there are many whites also involved. Violence has come out of this—not out of school or state policies on integration in Brooklyn.

This, in general, would, I believe, sum up the present administration attitude.

There is in it no hostility toward the South or its people, no wish to force anything, but there is a full determination to enforce due process of law—north, south, east, or west.

"The Judicial Power"

"THE judicial power of the United States shall be vested in one Supreme Court, and in such inferior courts as the Congress may from time to time order and establish."

"This Constitution and the laws of the United States which shall be made in pursuance thereof, and all treaties made, or which shall be made under the authority of the United States, shall be the supreme law of the land, and the judges in every State shall be bound thereby, anything in the Constitution or laws of any State to the contrary notwithstanding."

"The Senators and Representatives before mentioned, and the members of the several State Legislatures, and all executive and judicial officers, both of the United States and of the several States, shall be bound by oath or affirmation to support this Constitution."

"The Congress, whenever two-thirds of both Houses shall deem it necessary, shall propose amendments to this Constitution, or, on the application of the Legislatures of two-thirds of the several states, shall call a convention for proposing amendments, which in either case shall be valid to all intents and purposes, as part of this three-fourths of the several States, or by conventions in three-fourths thereof, as the one or the other mode of ratification may be proposed by the Congress."

34

These selections from the Constitution of the United States are, respectively, from Art. III, sec. 1; from Art. VI, secs. 2 and 3, and Art. V.

They are at issue in the court's deliberations following the arguments in the stay appeal from Little Rock. They may be helpful in public consideration of this grave issue.

There is valid reason to believe the Supreme Court will, in some manner, define its phrase "deliberate speed," contained in the decision of 1954. One believes this because it is, in effect, open at both ends. Five years have passed since it was handed down. The court may well feel it now should say what it meant.

The President of the United States said, taking the headlines away from his Department of Justice, that he felt there might be a slowing down. The U.S. Attorney General, voicing the White House policy, was drowned out by the presidential voice, almost incredibly proclaiming an opposite policy.

Illustrating the confusion in the administration, the brief filed by the Justice Department does not suggest any slowness. The Justice Department is a part of the executive. It would seem that here again the President doesn't know, or forgets, what is White House policy.

It asks, in effect, what do you mean by "slowing down"?

In seven states there has been no start at all. There have been instead, proclamations that there never will be a start. In other states affected there are some three thousand school districts and a start has been made in about seven hundred of them.

The Justice Department asked, in effect, Where has there been any speed? How can you slow down something which is at best crawling at tortoise speed? The Justice Department, which is a part of the executive, took this position about twelve hours after the President had said that he may have told a friend he thought the process might be slowed down.

Political writers in Washington have a word for this sort of thing, "butterfingers." A president who has no background of political experience is apt to be butter-fingered, always dropping fly balls or hard-hit grounders.

The court may define its phrase permitting a slower pace. But the Deep South and Governor Faubus, by defiance, make it difficult for the court so to do.

For the sake of our own thinking we must know that unless there is an amendment to the Constitution the court decision of 1954 is constitutional and binding on the courts, despite sincere disagreement. We have been hurt enough by those who have said it is unconstitutional. If the court gives more time it must be used intelligently.

Decision in Faubus Case

A UNITED STATES Court of Appeal sitting in St. Louis, Missouri, unanimously dismissed suits by Governor Orval Faubus, and others, against the government's actions in the Little Rock school case. At issue was the injunction against the governor's using state troops to oppose the district court's decree. The direct issue was whether the governor could use state troops to deny a court decree.

It should be plain, as was here repeatedly noted at the time, that any other decision would mean anarchy. If a governor, for example, can use state troops to defy the constitutional rulings and the law of the United States, he could, if he were power-drunk enough, use troops to close down newspapers which criticized him. He could shut churches whose ministers might incur the governor's dislike by putting troops around them.

If a governor can use troops to defy the federal law and the rights guaranteed under the Constitution, he can use them to forbid public assembly, freedom of speech, and all other rights of the citizens.

This was the issue—one of law. There were still legal moves which could have been initiated in the segregation case—but not defiance of a court.

This is precisely what the three-judge court has said, in an emphatic and unanimous decision. It held that the state of Arkansas could not lawfully use its state force to suppress rights which it is the duty of the state to defend.

The court said:

The use of troops or police for such purposes would breed violence. It would constitute an assurance to those who resort to violence to obtain their ends that if they gathered in sufficient numbers to constitute a menace to life, the forces of law would not only not oppose them but would actually assist them in accomplishing their objective.

Surely no fair-minded citizen, no matter what his personal feelings for or against the school case, can deny the soundness of this decision.

Now, let us go a bit farther.

It is proper to say that the violence in Jacksonville, Florida, where a synagogue and a Negro school were bombed, is the work of crackpots. That is true.

It is somewhat ironic, although not amusingly so, to find many of the same sources which denounced the government for acting to prevent anarchy, now are strongly denouncing the crackpots and lunatic-fringe bombers.

It is not amusing because, to a substantial degree, these dangerous fringe criminals are the product of those who so violently denounced the federal government for its insistence on upholding the decree of a federal court.

This certainly gave encouragement to those who are described as the lunatic and crackpot fringe. These persons are so described because they do not reason or think, and because they have no sense of citizenship or reverence for law. For persons and organizations in high places to give support to defiance of the court encourages all criminals.

Certainly it is proper strongly to dissent from the court's decisions—that of the schools or any other. It is proper, as was done in the issue of prohibition, to seek legislation which would reverse the court. It still is perfectly all right to do this. It is still the full right of a state to close its schools or to seek other orderly evasions of the law.

It is neither proper nor good Americanism, however, to encourage or approve defiance of the law. There was a great deal of this in the Little Rock case. It is this which produces the unamusing irony of seeing some of those who so encouraged disrespect for law and orderly procedure now so carefully drawing back their skirts from the violence done by the lunatic fringe. The two are inseparable.

The three-judge court has simply said that a state may not use its forces to suppress rights—any rights—which it is the state's duty to defend. Surely none of us, however we may feel about the school case, would wish any other decision.

Notes on Bastille Day

USUALLY in Paris it is only those American tourists who liked the *Tale of Two Cities,* or who have read Carlyle and others on the French Revolution, who go to the old quarter of Saint Antoine to see the site of Bastille.

There is not, in truth, much to see.

The revolutionists succeeded in capturing the old prison, once a fort, on July 14, 1789. It was not strongly defended, but even so would have held out had not some of the artillery forces in the city deserted to the rebels and begun a bombardment. The governor surrendered on promise of safety, but he was killed on the way to the Hotel de Ville and his head stuck on a pike.

On the following day the wreckage of the building was razed by the victory-crazed mobs. Today there is only the outline of the old structure, painted in a neat line of white paint. There is, about in the center, a lofty column of bronze dedicated to the martyrs of the revolutions of 1789 and of 1830.

The Bastille was, on July 14, 1789, and is now, a symbol of tyranny. It had long been a fortress for criminals and for those who had incurred the wrath of the kings. The prisoners were almost never brought to trial. They remained in the gloomy fortress all their lives. Some were put in as children. Many went there because they had offended one of the mistresses of the king or some promi-

40

nent person at the court. Some were placed in small cages, and kept there for long years.

Most of the better-known prisoners in the Bastille were writers sent there for criticizing the kings and their doings. It is a commonplace thread of history that, once persons come to power, they begin to think they are above criticism, and that it is somehow illegal to show up their knavery.

So, almost every journalist who goes to Paris journeys out to the site of the Bastille and stands there thinking and, maybe, dedicating himself to rebellion against tyranny. He buys flowers from one of the several old women who sell them thereabouts, places them on the base of the statue, and then goes into one of the small bistros in the neighborhood. There he drinks a "fine" to the revolutions of 1789 and of 1830 and goes on his way, a duty done. One who thinks there also recalls the words "responsibility" and "principle."

The French Revolution was much of a failure because it lacked any management, or executive direction. This has been, in a sense, the failure of France ever since. The excesses of unguided revolutionaries, and the tyranny of the dictators who followed, caused the republic to place the chief executive in a sort of political bastille.

In a sense, the French revolution was an outgrowth of the American. Some of those who had assisted the British colonies in North America to rebel and win their freedom were a part of the French rebellion which got so much out of hand. In America we had, though it may seem overly pious and smug to say so, a strain of morality in those leaders who directed our revolution. George Washington, Ben Franklin, John Adams, and all the others who were an integral part of it had before them the Declaration of Liberty.

In France in 1789 and the bloody years thereafter, until Napoleon came, the mob and all its outrages were tolerated. The most dreadful demagogues were allowed full sway. Massacre followed massacre. For two gore-smeared years the blood letting went on, matching any horror of the old Bastille.

History of this sort teaches those interested in freedom the importance of principle, and the necessity for citizens to observe as citizens the obligations of humanity and justice.

This can be the further simplified.

It is the old story of law and order. If we ever grow sympathetic toward the mob when it opposes the principles of justice and humanity, we too will destroy our system of government.

It is necessary to remember that the American Revolution had this principle from the very beginning and that the republic was based on it.

General Lee Reminds Us

IT was almost as if an innocent child had asked a question. But, it was no child. It was a woman with children.

On two successive days in the Deep South, in Georgia, two federal judges, both native to the state and each high in the esteem of the state population, had handed down antisegregation decisions.

The first was in the field of trolley and bus transportation. The second was in education. A unit of the state university system was notified by the court that segregation of qualified students was unconstitutional.

The call from the troubled lady was typical. She had heard the news on television. She telephoned to ask for more complete information and for verification. She was informed that the judge had, in fact, ruled that segregation of qualified students by reason of race or color was a violation of the federal law.

"But," she said, "the judge can't do that. Isn't it unconstitutional?"

There, revealed in all its innocence, was the dilemma of several millions of people in the Deep South. Much of their political leadership has from the start deceived them by saying that the Supreme Court of the United States has acted unconstitutionally. These same persons have argued, chiefly through attorneys making not inconsequential fees out of representing the states, that massive resistance will be sufficient answer to the "illegal" action of the high court.

These attorneys have received pompous advertising as "leading constitutional authorities."

What now has begun to happen in the Deep South is that local judges, "bone of our bone and flesh of our flesh," have begun to rule. The due processes of law are slow. Five years after a Supreme Court decision, native jurists in the various states have handed down decisions. They are judges familiar with Southern traditions. They are aware of the massive resistance. It is quite likely they are entirely out of sympathy with the 1954 decision.

Acting under oath and charged with supporting the Constitution, they are notifying the states involved that the government of the United States and its institutions of law are still in force. The Constitution, as interpreted by the Supreme Court, is a mandate on both state courts and federal.

This comes as a shock to many thousands of persons who have been fed everything but the truth.

Some of these leaders have urged upon the people of their states that they refuse "to surrender," as a matter of principle.

This overlooks a historical precedent, if anyone is interested.

It was the noble Robert E. Lee, hero to both the South and the North, who, against the advice and wishes of most of his staff, determined to surrender at Appomattox. He himself was heartbroken. But he said he knew further resistance could result only in greater harm to the South.

Because he loved the South more than he did his own career, his own feelings, his pride, he spent a night in prayer and then wrote out the offer of surrender.

He did not abandon his principles. He did not thereby say that he believed the opposition to be "right." He was first of all a man of integrity. Therefore, he surrendered to save the South further loss. Thereafter, until his death, he devoted himself to education, calling it the greatest Southern need.

General Lee was not a politician trying to protect himself in office against those who might thereafter claim he was "soft" in opposition to Yankees. Nor was he a lawyer earning a fee.

He had in mind his region, its people—and more particularly—its children of generations to come.

But, then, he was General Lee. Maybe it is true that we shall not look upon his like again.

The President as Professor

PRESIDENT DWIGHT D. EISENHOWER sought in his carefully prepared press statement to place the school integration issue within a clear framework of law. He reportedly was anxious that the White House position be made known well in advance of any school crisis.

The oath of a president—any president—is clear. He cannot avoid it. President Eisenhower, whatever his faults may be, has always been a stickler for duty. The responsibilities of his oath of office, and the oath itself, are an integral part of him, as they must be of any person of honor and integrity. The fact of his long military service makes him more sensitive to the word "duty."

It is understood that he sought, as he should have, advice from the Department of Justice. He worked carefully and personally on his statement. He feels that some of those who have been most defiant of the court have obscured the issue and made many people believe that the President may, by his own decision, take some other course. Apparently, some have been caused to believe the President himself is trying to force something upon them.

Behind the President's preparation of his statement was his intent to remind the people of their government and its functions.

It is the Supreme Court which was given the duty

of interpreting the Constitution of the United States. It has done this throughout the years. An interpretation allowed us to have selective service, social security, and many things not "in" the Constitution. Many persons strongly have attacked many decisions of the past as being unconstitutional. Some persons still regard them as so being. But they are not. The court has the clear right of interpretation of the Constitution. Only the Congress, in some cases, and the people by amendment in others, may change the effect of such interpretation.

There are many who violently disagree with the court on the school decision. They declare the court has acted unconstitutionally. Many of the persons who take this position are sincere. They honestly believe it. However right their legal arguments may be, the decision is constitutional. It will remain so until and unless the Congress shall adopt laws which reverse it; or until there is an amendment to the Constitution voted by the necessary states, which would reverse it. These are legal ways of so doing.

The President called on the states and their officials to tell the people the truth. He did not say so in such bold words. But he was rather plain. He said:

Each state owes to its inhabitants, to its sister states, and to the union the obligation to suppress unlawful forces. It [the state] cannot by action or deliberate failure to act permit violence to frustrate the preservation of individual rights as determined by a court decree. It is my hope that each state will fulfill its obligation with a full realization of the gravity of any other course. . . . Defiance of this duty would present the most serious problem, but there can be no equivocation

47

as to the responsibility of the federal government in such an event . . . the very basis of our individual rights and freedom rests upon the certainty that the President and the Executive branch of government will support and insure the carrying out of the decision of federal courts.

So said the President. He could not take a position of saying he would support the courts and the law in one case and not another.

The states have other legal courses open. Some are willing to pay the tragic price of closing their schools. That is legal. There are various other legal approaches which, while not legal if adopted for the purposes of evading law, will produce considerable delay. No state law in conflict with the federal is sovereign.

We can hope that no leader, state or local, will suggest violence.

It would be helpful, too, if the people would be told the truth. However regrettable it may be, and however much it goes against long-established customs and traditions—as it does—the court decision is constitutional until and unless changed by congressional act or constitutional amendment.

This was what the President asked from the states.

Once a Biscuit Is Opened

BACK in the days of minstrel shows there was one end man ballad singer whose specialty was titled, "I'm the Only Man in the World Who Can Take a Biscuit Apart and Put It Back Together Again Just Like It Was."

In a very real sense the inability to do just this is the dilemma of the Southern politicians. They have opened the Dixie biscuit for industry, labor unions, larger city populations and less rural, and yet they spend much of their time and emotions continually trying to put the biscuit back together again just like it was.

They can't. No matter how much of the molasses of tradition and recrimination they pour on it, it never will go back "just like it was."

They never blame themselves. As they angrily try to fit the old-time biscuit back together again, they blame the Supreme Court and Justice Warren. They accuse the vaguely defined "liberals" and the A.D.A. (Americans for Democratic Action). They are sure the Communists are yet another reason why the lid won't fit back on the biscuit.

Some of them are sure the poor fit of the biscuit is due to a Swedish sociologist who wrote a really understanding book on the nation's problems of race and titled it *The American Dilemma*. It was among the several publications referred to by the court, not as an authority on law but as one by a man who had studied the effect of unequal application of the laws. Almost none have read Gunnar Myrdal's book. But they blame him. Actually his book does not condemn the South. It argues that the problem is national, not regional.

If it isn't all these then surely it must be "the radicals" who prevent the biscuit from fitting together again.

All this the trained observer finds difficulty in comprehending. Every state, city, town, and chamber of commerce in the South for years have had both thumbs up, willing to attract industry from either, or any, direction. Governors of Southern states routinely take delegations of prominent citizens to large centers of industry to present—with oratory—diagrams and statistics revealing the water supply, the labor market, transportation, and the availability of public schools.

Once industry comes and the results become evident in new and unexpected pressures at the polls and in demands for services, there is contentment only with the payroll. Resentment grows against "outsiders" and "agitators from up North" who do not understand our way of life.

It is, as aforesaid, almost incomprehensible there should be such blindness, but there is.

Nor is that all. So fixed is attention on the problem of putting the biscuit top back again exactly as before there is no time for looking elsewhere and relating the great ferment of peoples everywhere for equal protection of law, for independence, and for status as God-made human beings. The explosions in Nyasaland, the Belgian Congo, Algeria, Cairo, and South Asia are associated with the impossible business of putting the lid back on the biscuit.

The astonishing spectacle of ministers of the gospel angrily defining Christianity as a segregated religion; the more understandable attempt of various councils, some business and professional men, and politicians all defiantly insisting they will put the biscuit top on just like it was —or destroy the biscuit—all this is almost incredible. It is more than that. It is preposterous and, for the generations of now and of the future, a demonstration filled with pathos and frustration.

The kindest thing is to say that it is most naïve to believe that after two great wars for liberty and the rule of law, and at a time when the American promise of equal protection for all citizens is being challenged by Communism, everything will go on as before. The American promise of dignity and equal application of the laws does not apply to a select classification of individuals. Socially they may do as they please. But the law must govern all equally in all public, non-private functions of life.

After Schools Close, Then What?

HOW strong is the devotion of the people to education and the public school?

This question, now that it has been, or soon will be, narrowed to "school or no school" in four of the fifty states, may not be answered for a long and agonizing span of time. Nowhere in the four states—Alabama, Georgia, South Carolina, and Mississippi—is local opinion free to act. Even if it were, the assumption is it would support the political leaders who declared the policy of complete resistance and obtained large majorities for it. The one exception is Virginia, though even there it is largely restricted.

Already, in Charlottesville, Norfolk, and Front Royal, Virginia, as in Little Rock, there are indications that a considerable number of parents and school children never understood that massive resistance would mean that schooling would end. They had believed the state leadership which told them the court had acted unconstitutionally. The assumption must remain, lacking any chance for local self-government or for the pupils involved to decide, that the adults in these states still prefer to abandon their schools rather than allow even one school district to make a try at compliance.

The question left, therefore, is what will be done when the schools close. One partial answer is, of course, the

52

parochial schools. In Virginia, for example, some 12,000 pupils have, for some time, been attending desegregated schools, ably conducted, as usual, by the Roman Catholic Church.

It is almost beyond belief that any state would sell off its school plants, valued at many millions of dollars and paid for by state taxes. But if one of the four should do this, it is certain that the Roman Catholic and the major Protestant churches—Episcopal, Lutheran, Methodist, Baptist, Presbyterian, Jehovah's Witnesses, and Seventh-Day Adventists—would buy some of the better and more modern plants.

At best, this would take up but a part of the slack. Such parochial schools would, for the most part, be in the larger centers of population. Here again it would be the rural areas and the small towns which would most likely become semieducational deserts.

There is another aspect of the problem which requires some planning. Teachers are human beings. Now that the private school plan has, as was inevitable, been declared illegal, there is sure to be a great outgoing of teachers. The younger ones especially will wish to make a career in states where the public school system is intact. Older teachers unable to move to another state will bear the brunt of chaos in their profession. There might be enough of these to staff a few of the better financed parochial schools. New teachers, of course, will not come into the states involved save to those parochial and private schools already in existence and to new ones which will mushroom up here and there.

Also ahead for the political leaders in the states which

plan to close schools when confronted with a court order is the very considerable matter of school bonds, the interest which must be paid on them, and the large debts of the school building authorities. Once schools are closed will the counties and cities continue to collect a school tax?

There are many other problems. Those of the children will be most acute. Our undisputed need is for more and better education—not less. A generation of children in four states will bear, unless the adults change their minds —as they are not likely to do—a heavy penalty. There can be no question but that the people voted by heavy majorities to close their schools if and when a court order is received. It is impossible to believe that many who so voted understood that it was a question of school or no school.

The real issue was never that of being for segregation or against it. It isn't now, save in the realm of politics. A great many people who hate the idea of even a "token" desegregation still believe in keeping the public schools open. But they are in the minority. There can be no question but that in four states the majority vote was to close the schools when confronted with a court order.

"Ninety Per Cent Are Lunatics"

ON the day that a grand jury here returned indictments against five men, all local, charging them with participating in the shocking dynamiting of the Temple early on Sunday morning, October 12, a disconsolate printer in Arlington, Virginia, made a historic statement.

It is one which, for lucidity and accuracy, deserves to be placed with the more revealing utterances of our time.

Printer Rockwell, who admires Hitler, is extremely anti-Jewish. He himself publishes much of the preposterous trash charging Jews with being traitors and malefactors. Printer Rockwell seemingly had been a pay-off man to some of the group in Atlanta. He mentioned, in a letter taken from one of those indicted, a "fat cat," who was providing most of the money for the hate operations.

From the letter one could read between the lines that the "fat cat" was regarded as a dupe and a fool. And, oh how they liked to spend the "fat cat's" money!

But to hasten on to Mr. Rockwell's historic statement. He was sad because his boys in Atlanta had become involved in charges of dynamiting.

"There is one great trouble with our [anti-Jewish] movement," he told the *North Virginia Sun*. "Ninety per cent of the people in the movement are lunatics."

While this may be on the conservative side, let us be

55

content with it. If anyone knows, it should be Rockwell. If out of his long association with this crowd he finds that 90 per cent of them are lunatics, we won't quarrel with the estimate.

What sort of claims does this rabid fringe pour into the mails to deceive the ignorant and the uninformed and to inflame the prejudiced?

Here's a sample. It is printed on yellow paper and is from the stuff being vended about the nation. It is a part of that turned up in Atlanta.

The Free Masons, Communists and New Deal Democrats are the "puppets" of the Jews in their horrible plot for world government . . . the Jew is organizing the hate directed at the white race by the Negro . . . and more especially against our fair Southland . . . against white America. Christ's way is Faubus' way . . . the Jews work against God.

There is more of this weird, fantastic stuff. Tons of it are mailed out each year, and—God help us—there are those fevered brains which accept it.

The indictments and the revelations that there are other groups about the country and that they have a loosely knit organization financed by the secretly laughed-at "fat cats," should have other results.

They may be listed:

1. There were those, including a national columnist or so, who tried to put over the propaganda that the dynamiting was not the act of any native group operating in the South, but was a deep Communist plot directed by Moscow. There were also even more ridiculous suggestions that Negroes or Jews did the bombings. This was

fantastic but it was assiduously peddled. One can only assume these people want to divert attention from the fact that the anti-Semitic groups are also active in racial agitation and make consistent use of it. The Communists are an ever-present danger, but they are by no means all of it.

2. Those accused, and all others of like mind, all native Southerners, are encouraged by the attitude of Southern leaders who have preached, not disagreement, but violent resistance to the Supreme Court authority and the processes of law. There is a great difference—a complete difference—between loudly disagreeing with decisions by the courts and the act of denying the authority of the courts and the law. We can all disagree openly and strongly. But those of us who flaunt authority of the courts thereby encourage all those who are eager to carry out violence and destruction.

"Know Thy Adversary!"

ONE of the truest of the old axioms is, "Know thy adversary!"

Americans almost desperately need to know the Communist adversary. They have heard from the extremists in race that the Supreme Court proclaims Communist doctrines in its decisions. They have heard the anti-Semites say that the Jews spread Communism. They have heard that the civil rights bills are Communistically inspired.

These lies, repeated over and over again, have given to many an honest and well-meaning person a confusion of mind easily understandable. This propaganda appears in the hate sheets sent out by the various organizations devoted to hate.

The Congress of the United States, in the Dies Committee and in later investigations by other House committees on un-American affairs, has issued a number of reports on this subject. One of the latest, "Neo-Fascist and Hate Groups," prepared and released by the Committee on Un-American Activities, U.S. House of Representatives, says in the first paragraph:

Communism's present threat to the very survival of the United States and the rest of the free world has placed heavy burdens on the defenders of human freedom and dignity. The Committee on Un-American Activities is concerned to observe that this burden is being aggravated by certain individuals and organizations unscrupulously exploiting the menace of communism to promote other activities equally un-American."

The Un-American Affairs Committee then specifies such unscrupulous exploiting methods and lists as one the "organized hate group," "which masquerades as a defender of our republican form of government, yet conducts hate campaigns against racial and religious minorities in the infamous tradition of fascist dictatorships."

The report also names some of the notorious individuals and publications.

None can argue the House Un-American Activities Committee of the Congress is Communistically inspired. The mail is full of the sort of poisonous lies it describes. It comes on little four-page "newspapers" or one-page handbills. It may be mimeographed. It always is abusive of the Supreme Court, of Jews, Catholics, Negroes, educators, or some other group which such persons wish to revile.

These organizations, as the Congressional committee says, always pretend to defend the republic. They always have high-sounding patriotic names.

They have become so evil and so full of subversive lies that the government is being asked to bar their worst publications from the mail.

Hate and lies supporting it are stones tossed into a pool. The ripples wash up on the shores of dynamited synagogues, churches, and homes. Who will be next? Quakers, Roman Catholics, Baptist meetinghouses, Methodists? Jehovah's Witnesses already have felt the force of explosives.

Hate is never satisfied. Those who feed on it are like narcotic addicts. They always want more.

None of these persons of hate have ever been harmed or injured by a Jew, Negro, or any of the persons who stand for law as against defiance of it. What is the evil which drives them to abuse and violence?

It is high time that the United States government acted. There is no reason at all why the national organization of these hoodlums should not come under the scrutiny of the FBI. We have given that power in the crime of kidnaping and stealing automobiles. Are human lives and churches no more valuable?

America has something which no Communist country has—freedom and dignity for the individual. It presently is being eroded. The stuff poured out by the anti-Semitic haters, the Negro haters, and the Catholic haters is as dangerous to America as that of the Communist publications. And it is the more deceitful. It masks itself in patriotism.

Educate Only the Well To Do?

PERHAPS the most significant feature of the various "private school plans" being proposed in the few Southern states still planning on complete resistance to even token desegregation of a few schools is the slowly dawning realization that such schools will be available only to the children of parents who can afford $250 to $500—or more—per year per pupil.

Politicians who embrace these features to educate the children of the rich and well to do and leave illiterate and unprepared for life those of the poor may live to have political regrets.

The states have a legal right to have no school system at all. But as Governor Almond of Virginia has indicated, the various state laws, including those of private schools financed by the state, are almost certainly unconstitutional in their entirety. Governor Almond and state school leaders also are well aware, as most parents are not, that the average state financial assignment to pupils, if finally permitted by the courts, would be less than $250 in each of the states where massive resistance prevails. This they know, as the average parent does not, is not nearly enough to support adequate schools. It would encourage the mushrooming of hundreds of schools for profit only, most of which would be in the hands of unscrupulous promoters.

Until recently there has been a feeling, "Oh, well, the

61

political leadership will work it out . . . they won't really kill our public schools."

A Virginia editor has summed up rather well what is a new state of mind now found in the states committed to massive and complete resistance to the U.S. Supreme Court's school decision and the several subsequent rulings by lower courts.

"The people did not understand," he wrote, "that when the candidates for office were assuring them that 'if you elect me there will be no desegregation,' the candidates really were saying 'if you elect me there will be no schools.' "

Georgia's Senator Herman Talmadge, in a press conference just before departing for Europe and a NATO meeting, stirred the people of the Deep South by predicting a closing of the schools and by having no ready remedy to offer.

This rather effectively disposed of the feeling entertained by many that their state leadership would somehow "work it out" and manage to maintain the public schools.

Despite protest and wishful thinking on the part of many, it slowly and painfully becomes plain that we are, after all, a government by law and not of men. Until laws are upset and the system of courts overturned, we must proceed by due processes of laws.

Many parents, while fully approving and supporting public schools, have always preferred, for reasons of religious instruction, or small classes, the private school.

The truly private school is perfectly legal. It must be genuinely so, and it will be, at best, expensive.

The public school system, into which so much money and devotion have been poured, is everywhere crowded and in need of classrooms. To assume that a private system suddenly could be set up in private buildings and the educational needs fulfilled is, of course, an impossibility.

Indications now are that in the end only four states of the fifty will go to the extreme of abolishing their schools. This they have a perfect right to do.

Out of the chaos of no schools and the attempt to establish a private system will emerge a public school system. A period of years may well intervene. The new system may even be a federally supported one born of necessity. There will, in time, be public schools, for the reason that the nation cannot afford to be without them. This is the twentieth century. It is the era of great scientific advances and new technologies. It is the time of increasing urbanization. It is a period when more educated people, not fewer, are needed. We cannot escape from the twentieth century.

There is just one—and only one—ready solution. It is for the local boards to be given the right of decision. Where that is refused, there is no chance to avoid a court order.

If We Ask the Missionaries

SINCE the beginnings of the Populist-Agrarian revolution of the latter part of the nineteenth century, the dominant symbol in American politics has been "the common man."

It now is quite clear that we are in the beginnings of an era in which the most powerful symbol of world politics is, and will increasingly be, "the colored man." World emphasis may well shift to Africa itself and remain there for a considerable span of time as the Communist plotters of Russia pursue what seems opportunity.

It is almost a calamity, insofar as American public opinion is concerned, that all our newspapers could not publish a full account of the first all-African peoples conference at Accra, Ghana.

There was hope in it for the West. There was evidence that a revised foreign policy is necessary. There was a small harvest from the visit to Africa by Vice President Nixon two years ago. The fact that Israel has established trade and technical exchanges with Ghana was also reflected.

Ghana's Prime Minister Kwame Nkrumah keynoted the meeting. He reminded African leaders that threats of colonialism and imperialism might come in a "different guise," not necessarily from Europe. It was a clear warn-

64

ing against Communism and the ambitions of Egypt's Nasser.

But it was Tom Mboya, an anti-Communist labor leader from Kenya, who said what Americans, in particular, will find helpful in trying to understand the forces at work in Africa.

Our image of Africa is one of missionaries, elephants, big-game hunters, and a gentle old man with drooping mustaches—Dr. Schweitzer.

That it is a continent covering one fifth of the earth's surface, an area larger than China, India, and the United States combined, somehow startles us.

Tom Mboya perhaps would have amused some of the Western audience. He stood before the conference, reported the New York *Times'* Kenneth Love, wearing a beaded tribal hat, a lionskin pouch, and a dark, double-breasted blue suit. He spoke to a captivated audience, which cheered madly this comment:

Some have said Africans are not yet ready to be free. Others have said we are not civilized enough. To this we give a simple answer:

Civilized or not civilized, ignorant or illiterate, rich or poor, we, the African states, deserve a government of our own choice. Let us make our own mistakes, but let us take comfort in the knowledge that they are our own.

There must be majority rule in Africa as in America. Even in the Union of South Africa the question is not whether Africans will win. It is how and when. The people must be organized into militant mass organizations.

We will not tolerate any attempt by any country—and that means any—to undermine the independence that we are fighting for. We shall never sell our freedom for capital or technical assistance.

That African nations will be formed and attain independence is sure. The big problem is our policy. It should not be overlooked that the declaration of union between Ghana and Guinea began "Inspired by the example of the American colonies."

Our heritage is one of revolution to win independence. Many of us now forget that fact.

The British, of all colonial powers, have done the best job. British Africa is twenty times as large as Britain. Ghana is a former colony. Nigeria is to be independent in another year. French Africa covers an area also twenty times as large as France. Belgian Africa is one hundred times the size of Belgium. Portuguese Africa has an area twenty-one times that of Portugal. Spanish Morocco is as large as New Jersey.

The same forces which made over the map of Asia are at work in Africa.

Does anyone wonder why our own racial problem is of meaning beyond our borders? Do Christian church congregations know what their missionaries are saying?

A Lesson We Can Learn

I F WE will, we can learn a valuable lesson from the crisis brought on by the struggle to prevent Arab nationalism from being subverted by the Communists.

A better word for this nationalism is "Pan-Arabianism." "Pan" is from the Greek. It means "all," or "universal"; the familiar "Pan-American" is a good example. Iraq's new government has not yet affiliated with the United Arab Republic as originated and ruled by Egypt's President Nasser. In its first announcement of government, however, Iraq said it belongs to the "Arab Nation." It clings to the idea of Pan-Arabia.

The Communists have not merely endorsed this idea; they have supported Nasser with weapons and money. They have contributed to the Communists in all possible countries in the Middle East. They applaud the rebels of Iraq. This is the typical Communist technique of riding any movement which seems likely to upset the *status quo* in the Middle East—or in any other part of the world. They hope to be able to get a foothold, and if they should, they would quickly get rid of the present Arab leadership—including Nasser.

It is important that we understand that as of now the great emotional force of Arab nationalism for Pan-Arabia is not Communist. The Commies support it for cynical, practical reasons.

From this we can learn a lesson at home. Our problem of race is an old one. It has grown slowly but steadily across the bygone years, as Negro citizens sought to live under the equal protection of the law in all public fields of national life. The courts have ruled there can be no discrimination between citizens.

It was inevitable that the Communist party should do in our country exactly what they have done in the Middle East. They gave loud support to the court's finding.

All Americans, whether pro or con with regard to the court decision, owe it to themselves to understand that it is not a Communist movement any more than is Nasser's. We live in a time of complex problems and confusion. It does not make sense to deceive and confuse ourselves, or to permit others to do it for us. Whatever one may think or feel about it, it is not Communism to aspire to the equal protection of the Constitution and the laws of our country. This aspiration on the part of the Negro citizenship would exist if there were no Russia, just as Arab nationalism was in full cry in 1916 before there was a Communist revolution in the Czar's Russia.

Whatever we may feel about it, or do about it, it is important to know that. It is a Communist technique to make a people distrust themselves, their government, and their courts. That any of us in this nation, which is so determined to resist the evil of Communism, should allow anger or prejudice to accept for a minute the preposterous, un-American suggestion that court members are Communistic or are influenced by Russia, as some of our more angry persons have charged, is unworthy of us.

We can be angry and resentful, and we can seek to

have the court decision reversed. We can have our representatives in Congress initiate counterlegislation. Any legal avenue is open to attack the court. But no person of common sense will harbor the Communist suggestion. It delights the Communists, of course, to have our more demagogic personalities make such attacks. Communism profits thereby.

The way ahead, at home and internationally, is going to be one of hardship, danger, and trial of all that is best in us and our form of government. Loyalty to America is a necessary ingredient of that future. We can thank God that Communism does not attract more than a handful of Americans. The Negro, for all the effort by Communists to attract him because of the many discriminations, has had relatively few turncoats. But Communism persists and will remain an ever present danger. We can learn a lesson from the Middle East and not permit Communists, whom J. Edgar Hoover properly has called "Masters of Deceit," to make us doubt ourselves and our institutions. Our problem of race is an American problem. It is, in fact, 100-per-cent American.

Whose States Rights?

NOW and then one of the more antiquated of the extreme states rights tribes within the Democratic party will beat his breast like a Tarzan and demand a return to the philosophy of Jefferson and Jackson.

This is odd. Jefferson made it very plain in his great message to the Congress in 1806, that he would not forever keep the nation in the strait jacket of the original constitutional restraints.

Jefferson emphasized that to him the Constitution was not a fetish to be worshiped. Those were his words. He said it should not be made sacrosanct against change. It was, he said, an instrument for service to the nation, to be changed when changed conditions demanded change in the interest of progress.

Andrew Jackson, when John C. Calhoun attempted the policy of interposition and invoked states rights, informed him the Union and its sovereignty would be preserved if he had to send 50,000 troops there to do it and arrest and hang Calhoun as a traitor.

Jefferson was no standpatter. And no one ever suggested such about Old Hickory.

Governor LeRoy Collins of Florida currently seems to be the one Southern governor who is talking sense to the people on the subject of states rights.

He said:

There is much talk these days about "states rights." The term seems to have a variety of meanings, depending on who is doing the talking. I believe there are areas of service where the states should have the full responsibility, and that it would be a good thing for the country if the governmental domains of the states and the national government were more clearly delineated. This, however, can never be easy to accomplish.

There followed these pertinent and bold paragraphs:

So when we think of "states rights" we should bear in mind that the paramount American democratic concern historically has been for the rights of people rather than the rights of government, whether national or state. And I submit that the measure of worth of any level of American government is the degree to which it approaches that goal.

Just as it should not meddle where individuals or private interests are doing the job well, so should government never hesitate to act boldly and imaginatively in those fields where individuals are unable or unwilling to get the necessary job done.

Government is the people's business. As such, it must be dedicated to the public interest. And the public interest can never be measured by the sum total of the special interests.

Government should be a dynamic and creative force in our society, not a disinterested bystander or a blind referee or a passive *status quo* caretaker, for the American people will always be a dynamic people with ever-changing needs.

Governor Collins noted that the joint State-Federal Action Committee, created by the President in an effort to return projects to the states, had found it impossible

71

to unscramble the omelette of existing joint federal-state programs.

The recommendations by the committee of programs to be returned to the states constitute less than 2/100 of one per cent of the money now expended by the national government in support of state and local services.

We are faced, as Governor Collins said, with the burden of rundown and neglected facilities due to failure of state government in past years to face up to responsibilities.

We also face a second problem: How to provide facilities to accommodate the needs of today's population. These are two staggering problems.

The cry of states rights by those whose states have failed in their responsibilities to the people is less and less valid.

States Rights, State Failures

IN the often grotesque exaggerations which occur in the Deep-South debate over the life or death of the public school system, the phrase most often used by those who lack facts or logic is the ambiguous one of "states rights."

This is all the more unreal because historians are agreed that it was the compulsive determination of the Confederate states to make states rights and slavery "the cornerstone of their edifice" which doomed it. A central authority was required to wage a war. There was so little of it that the states pulled in many directions on almost all major issues. Military and economic ruin was inevitable.

In his famous test with John C. Calhoun in 1833, Andrew Jackson forced the South Carolinian to drop his attempt at interposition of state sovereignty versus federal. The War Between the States settled the issue permanently. The federal law must be supreme, or there is no possibility of government.

Since 1865 the states have all but abandoned those reserve rights, such as building their own highways, hospitals, health departments, et cetera. They have, of necessity, turned to the central government to take over many state responsibilities. This often is regrettable. Local government is preferable, but government cannot stand still if the states are unable to act. There will be more and more turning to the federal government as population demands increase.

There already is a grievous disparity of opportunity. The people of some states have higher quality of education, health facilities, roads, and communications. People will not and should not be expected to accept this merely to sustain the usually specious and entirely political use of an ambiguous phrase, "states rights."

Governor LeRoy Collins of Florida, whose state has excelled all its neighbors in population growth and per capita income increase, recently quoted Elihu Root. Almost half a century ago Root, who headed Woodrow Wilson's mission to Russia, said of the so-called doctrine of states rights:

It is useless for the advocates of states rights to inveigh against the supremacy of the constitutional laws of the United States or against the extension of national authority in the fields of necessary control where the states themselves fail in the performance of their duty.

The instinct for self-government among the people of the United States is too strong to permit them long to respect anyone's right to exercise a power which he fails to exercise. The governmental control which they deem just and necessary they will have.

It may be that such control would better be exercised in particular instances by the governments of the states, but the people will have the control they need, either from the states or from the national government, and if the states fail to furnish it in due measure sooner or later constructions of the constitution will be found to vest the power where it will be exercised—in the national government.

74

This convincing analysis exactly fits the present crisis. The states utterly failed to carry out the separate but equal decision. State failure to meet this responsibility, plus the march of history and other developments in the field of human rights, produced a constitutional construction "to vest the power where it will be exercised."

Today's problems include those of great, costly magnitude. Just as the states turned eagerly to the federal government to assume their responsibilities in the great depression, so will they of necessity turn to Washington for help in meeting them.

A state cannot continue half-responsible and half-irresponsible. Nor can it pick and choose as to what "rights" it will insist on this year and which it will abandon next year.

A Plea for Simple Truth

THIS is really an essay about judges—especially those of the federal system.

There was a historic feature to the Federal District Court decision declaring all segregated school systems in violation of the Fourteenth Amendment not contained in previous decrees in any other state.

In it one got a picture of the loneliness of judges who, once they take what is one of the most solemn of oaths, must withdraw from much of life. They also must seal their lips insofar as any comment on politics or public controversy is concerned.

Only in their decisions may they reveal some of their repressed emotions. Then they can do so only in the calm judicial phrases which explain their decisions.

Since the 1954 United States Supreme Court decision a great many persons have wondered if justices of state supreme courts, as well as members of the federal judiciary, were not sickened by all the deliberate deception of a disturbed, confused people who, in great majority, strongly opposed and dissented from the Supreme Court's constitutional interpretation of the Fourteenth Amendment.

They had to remain silent while men who knew better shouted that states rights were superior to the federal. They could say nothing while the utter nonsense of "interposition" was preached by men who argued a state could interpose its authority between the court and the federal government.

State Supreme Court justices and federal judges were mute while self-proclaimed authorities on the Constitution heatedly denounced the court and told a hopeful people, desperately seeking an escape, that the court was wrong and had acted unconstitutionally.

One felt a certain sympathy for the political leader who knew better, but who needed time to save face and somehow manage to tell the people the truth.

Many did so manage. They did let the people know that the Supreme Court decision was an established fact and would not be reversed. They attacked the decision, bitterly and angrily, as they had every right to do. But they didn't lie to the people about the primacy of the courts and law.

Then there were the smearers and the extremists who spoke of the President and the court and all who told the truth in terms most vulgar and foul.

Through all of this there was a silence by the justices of the higher courts, state and federal. It had to be. That silence will, of course, continue.

Now and then in court decisions one can read between the lines. In the Georgia decision the court announced it was, of course, bound by the Supreme Court, as are all other courts, state and federal. It noted that state legislatures had themselves admitted the fact the United States Supreme Court ruling constitutes the law on the question by passing laws seeking to meet the problems created by the decision.

The court then said that racially segregated schools

violated the Fourteenth Amendment to the Constitution of the United States.

There followed the historic feature, which has not appeared in any previous one. It seems inescapably a plea to leadership not to deceive the people further. The court said of its decision:

To make any other ruling would only add to the confusion which already exists in the minds of so many of our good citizens, and to build up in the breasts of our citizens hopes of escape which would soon be torn to shreds by rulings of our appellate courts on review. This court feels that any such ruling could accomplish no good, but only cause irreparable harm to our state and her people.

The deceptions and smearings of the past have already done great and lasting harm. One does not blame the people. They looked to their leaders. That was proper. Surely, from now on, whether that leadership determines to abolish its school system entirely, or to permit local decisions, it will tell the people the plain, simple truth. They have earned it.

Violence Destroys Its Own Purposes

THREE Klansmen have been sentenced to jail in North Carolina. They were caught with dynamite bombs, and the jury decided they were, as the evidence said, proceeding with a plot to blow up an elementary school. A member of the klavern who testified for the state said the plot grew out of disappointment over failure to obtain publicity by a cross-burning. Witnesses testified it was racial in origin.

Within the past weeks there have been dynamitings of synagogues and churches. Let us not blind ourselves to the reason for this. What we are getting is the fruit of the tree, even as the scriptures tell us.

It is the right of everyone who feels like it to criticize the Supreme Court. No one has ever denied that. One may deplore and criticize all one wishes. But we have had many men, some in high places, who have gone further than deploring or criticizing. They have, in fact and in effect, defied the court and denounced it in reckless, unscrupulous charges. Some have been reckless and false enough to charge Communism. We actually have had, here and there, some minor judges who publicly and for political reasons announced they would defy the court.

What do these men think this inspires ignorant and vicious men to do? It encourages them to violence of the sort we are having—bombings. It always does do that. It always will.

This newspaper insists we must be a nation of law. We can criticize the courts; we can deplore their decisions; we can seek by legal and legislative means to have their decisions reversed or amended.

No sound American citizen will encourage defiance of any court. We have had a lot of it, and some of it has come, and comes, from high places. It ought to stop. If it does not, then we will proceed to more and more lawlessness. That is the termite which destroys representative government.

There is a place in America—as always—for criticism and for all legal efforts to reverse or amend court decisions or to eliminate them by legislation.

There is no place for reckless defiance—and encouragement of such defiance.

Byrd Machine Knocked Out

V IRGINIA'S Byrd machine, which was the crude name for the aristocratic oligarchy which for so long has ruled Virginia, is broken.

It has by no means done a Humpty-Dumpty. It may be put together again in a form somewhat resembling the old one by Governor J. Lindsay Almond. But the Byrd machine has been knocked out.

The people of Virginia did it by voting for public schools. There should be a lesson in this for all politicians in all states where the issue remains. No political organization was more soundly based than that of Senator Harry Byrd.

The machine suffered its first defeat in history in the spring of 1959 in a special legislative session. Governor Almond called it to put before it his plan to allow the various communities in the state to decide whether they wanted to retain public schools or abandon them. The Byrd machine, which had instituted the shameful "massive resistance" program, fought him bitterly and with all the weapons of influence and demagoguery. Governor Almond won by the margin of a single vote.

But in mid-summer the people voted.

The Byrd forces of massive resistance centered their greatest effort on the Senate where the Almond margin was one. They lost all four seats. Nor was the margin of their loss a small one. Byrd's greatest hope was in Arlington. He was defeated by more than two to one.

This was the voice of the people.

They voted for public education—or at least for the right to have it if they wish it. At any rate, they voiced their determination to have local option and not to be told what to do by men who wanted to abandon education.

This is a historical victory. The Byrd machine was weighed in the balance. It didn't weigh as much as it thought. Certainly it could not outweigh public education.

Here the nation has a very clear view of the complex Southern problem. It is one of leadership. When the Supreme Court decision came down in 1954 the original reaction was one of stunned surprise and dissent, but also one of acceptance of constitutional decisions by the court.

There was a lull. It was one almost of silence. The more rabid extremists knew their voices were not strong or respected enough to lead. It was precisely at this moment that Senator Byrd threw the great weight of Virginia's magnificent tradition behind massive, total resistance.

Here began the great tragic deception of the Southern people.

They might have lacked full confidence in their own leadership, but Virginia was the state of origin of the Constitution, of the Bill of Rights, of religious liberty, of Jefferson and many of the great of our revolutionary history.

If Virginia says so, said many in the South, it must be so. So there spread rapidly and fanatically the dangerous and false theory of interposition and defiance which already have brought so much grief to so many Southern people. The worst of the demagogues, the ugliest of passions and prejudices were given dignity and status by the stand of the Byrd machine.

Late last year, Governor Almond of Virginia, realizing that the state could not prosper and endure without public education, decided to risk his political future by telling the truth. He informed the people they had been deceived. He told them the federal law and courts were superior in authority to those of the states. He told them desegregation could be controlled—as it can. It was a daring, honorable act of great statesmanship.

When his legislature met this past spring he knew he might be defeated. He won because there were enough men in the legislature who put their state and its future ahead of their political careers.

Now the people of Virginia, given the chance, have given notice that they too know the truth.

The story is one of leadership.

In What Fire Was Thy Brain?

RICHARD V. SMITH, JR., eighteen, has been sentenced to serve six to ten years in prison for having destroyed valuable paintings in the Columbus, Georgia, art museum because, he said, he believed them to be the work of Jewish artists. The young man definitely informed court officials that he considered the late Adolf Hitler to be "the reincarnation of whatever divine source that may exist," a statement which must have startled even the shade of that fateful Führer, at whatever level of hell it now dwells.

The young man also admitted painting swastikas on synagogues as a nocturnal recreation.

The solicitor general, however, reveals the young man as having been motivated by the impulses of a common thief, or burglar, rather than by those lofty or divine. He had, he said, broken into the museum to rob it, but finding no cash, set fire to the paintings.

His attorney describes him as a frustrated, confused lad. It is a bit difficult to understand frustration, but confused he is, though it is a kind word.

His attorney is without question more nearly accurate when he says his client has been "brainwashed by older persons." He did not name them. No one would question this belief. The young man obviously had fallen in with those who operate from the cesspools of hate from which are spewed out the various, though similar, publications filled with hatred and lies. They incite older persons to violence. What they might do to young unstable minds is at once obvious. You get a quick look into at least a partial explanation of some of the teen-age crime and violence in reading the story of eighteen-year-old Richard Smith. His story makes one think of Blake's "The Tiger."

> Tiger, Tiger, burning bright
> In the forests of the night,
> What immortal hand or eye
> Could frame thy fearful symmetry?
>
> . . . .
>
> What the hammer? what the chain?
> In what furnace was thy brain?
> What the anvil? what dread grasp
> Dare its deadly terrors clasp?

Young Smith's story as reported at the trial is a brief textbook on hate.

There is in Columbus, as in Atlanta, one of those publishing cesspools manufacturing dangerous narcotics of hate for sick minds.

The arresting officer said that young Smith had admitted activity with hate organizations in both these cities. One of the jobs which older persons gave him was to sneak their printed exhalations of hate between pages of books in the public libraries. He told them, too, that hate literature published in Columbus was distributed to other parts of the country, much of it going to troubled Little Rock.

One may simply put two and two together and know immediately why there are so many young hoodlums active in the mobs and disorders at Little Rock. They have been reading the literature which young Smith, and others, mailed out.

I remember writing, some years ago, about a man who had been arrested and convicted of being a party to a Ku Klux Klan killing. I suggested his early record indicated he was a good man and father. His tearful wife telephoned.

"Oh," she said, sobbing, "he was. He was a good man until those wicked men played on his vanity and made him think it would be a great thing to help beat this man. We couldn't talk to him after they got to him. It was awful. Awful."

You feel a sadness about the young Smiths of this world and their innocent families, who suffer agony. But for the evil men who cynically produce the hate publications, which they themselves don't believe, to make a profit out of the psychotic and sick of mind, there is only contempt.

As young Smith's attorney said—those really guilty of burning the paintings are those grownups who brainwashed him and took his money—and sent him to jail for six to ten years.

We Now Trust Our Youth

I T IS pleasant to note that the U.S. government has learned to believe in its young people. Or as the phrase has it, "our youth."

"Our youth" has fought a lot of battles for us. Again the cliché is at hand. On the land, the sea, and in the air they have proved themselves the heroic defenders of their flag and heritage.

Now, the government is delighted with itself for having learned that they equally are trustworthy out of uniform.

A year ago the United States put all possible obstacles in the way of typically curious, interested American youth asking permission to attend the Communist-dominated "World Youth Festival" which was scheduled for Moscow. It was, to be sure, a rather shocking revelation of a free country's fears about the ability of its citizens— especially the young—to appreciate and value freedom over Communist totalitarianism. It almost certainly was a carryover of the hysteria and doubt created by the late Senator Joe McCarthy.

At any rate, a number of American "youth" did attend the festival. Only a very few made asses of themselves. A somewhat embarrassed government of the United States was delighted at how well the great majority conducted themselves. They learned a lot. They held their own in the debates and questionings. The tricky Communists' dialectic did not confuse or dismay them. They made friends on the wonderful basis of being young together.

This was not all. The U.S. young people brought back no "intelligence" reports, but they did come back to write articles for their college papers and to give interviews to their home press which made sense and which gave a good idea of Moscow and of what went on there during the festival. It was a good "egghead" job.

This summer the festival is to be held in Vienna. It will, as before, be Communist dominated. This year, however, the government is encouraging interested college students to go ahead. The State Department is urging all who plan to go to study and acquaint themselves with the propaganda, the questions, and the needling to which they will be subjected.

There is no danger of the American egghead, youth or adult, being won over by Communism. Being an egghead, he is rather well informed. He has read, not merely Pasternak, but Jefferson—and for that matter, Chief Justice Warren. The immature bubblehead, who is at best shallow and who is looking for authority and someone to provide him with the "answers" to life, may find the Communist line romantic and fascinating. But, as the State Department learned, Joe McCarthy was wrong. The American colleges are not hotbeds of Communism. They are hotbeds of discussion, debate, and curiosity about life and people. We had best hope, for the sake of our country, they stay that way.

The youth of this country has its eyes open. It is looking rather closely at its leadership these days, as are a great many adults. The youth of the South is comparing the leadership which wants to close the public school system and make a farce of education with that which would save it and strengthen it. Youth everywhere is watching its political leaders cope with the new problems of urbanization, of unemployment. It is noting too their efforts to make opportunity for education available to all who earn.

The more mature American college student knows that change is all about him. He wants to know about it. He does not think of the federal Constitution as static and rigid. He suspects those who use it as an argument for maintaining any special privilege *status quo*. He prefers to be a part of the future of his country, not its past.

He will fight for his country against its enemies, and he is just as interested in defending its great principles of freedom and individual liberty in debate or discussion with a Communist youth. It's good the government has learned this.

The Slow Mills of Law!

O N A Friday, in June of 1959, in Atlanta, the due processes of law which began in May, 1954, with all deliberate speed, reached a time of decision for Georgia. Since we are a nation of law, the district court handed down the only possible decision. A segregated school system violates the Fourteenth Amendment.

The processes of law will continue. But they will do so with all deliberate speed.

It is important to know what, and why, the court decided as it did. The essential statement was this:

This court is bound by the decision of the United States Supreme Court as announced not only in the Brown case, but in many other cases subsequent to the Brown case, arising in Little Rock, Arkansas, in Virginia, and in other localities. Even the most ardent segregationists in the land, though bitterly opposed to such ruling, now recognize that racially segregated public schools are not permitted by law. Even the Legislature of Georgia and of other states recognize that the ruling of the United States Supreme Court constitutes the law on this question, and the various legislatures for some years have been passing laws in order to meet the problems created by such decisions. The validity of such laws is not now before this court for a decision. This court cannot at this time make any other ruling except a ruling to the effect that the operation of racially segregated public schools in

Atlanta violates the Fourteenth Amendment to the United States Constitution. To make any other ruling would only add to the confusion which already exists in the minds of so many of our good citizens, and to build up in the breasts of our citizens hopes of escape which would soon be torn to shreds by rulings of our appellate courts on review. This court feels that any such ruling could accomplish no good, but only cause irreparable harm to our state and her people.

This portion of the ruling, here given at some length, is a great contribution to common sense. The two Southern judges are both highly respected natives of the state where their decision applies.

In calm judicial language they rebuked those extremists in and out of politics who have for so long deliberately deceived the people by building up false hope of avoiding the processes of law. From the moment the Supreme Court ruled in 1954 there has been only one possible decision for the states to make. They can accept the provisions for slow change, or they can close the public school system. In obeying a state does not have to flood its schools with Negro children. It can, when it makes up its mind to have public schools, screen pupils and keep integration at a minimum. The court long ago confirmed this.

So it is that two judges, of complete integrity, had to say, rebuking all those who have cruelly deceived the people with talk of the court's having acted illegally and of states' rights being greater than those of the nation:

"To make any other ruling would only add to the confusion" . . . and would "build up in the breasts of our citizens hopes of escape which would soon be torn to shreds by rulings of our appellate courts."

This was never a question of being for integration or against it. It was, and is, a question of public schools or no schools. The court will provide time. The schools will hardly be closed this fall. But Georgia's legislature must determine whether it wants to end public education or adopt a placement law and continue it.

We shall see, in the months ahead, who will serve the future of the children and the state. We cannot afford to waste time on angry shoutings. The district court allows time for planning. The state can close all schools or allow the people in each community to decide what they wish —as Viginia has done.

But time is a-wastin'.